CAMBRIDGE IBERIAN AND
LATIN AMERICAN STUDIES

GENERAL EDITOR
P. E. RUSSELL F.B.A.
Emeritus Professor of Spanish Studies
University of Oxford

ASSOCIATE EDITORS
E. PUPO-WALKER
Director, Center for Latin American and Iberian Studies
Vanderbilt University
A. R. D. PAGDEN
Lecturer in History, University of Cambridge

An Introduction to the Politics and Philosophy of José Ortega y Gasset

This is the first book in English to provide a general survey of
the life and work of the Spanish philosopher and essayist Ortega
y Gasset (1883–1955), author of the widely-read *The Revolt of the
Masses*. Dr Dobson divides his study into sections devoted to
Ortega's political thinking and to his philosophy, rooting these
in the context of contemporary Spain and discussing the wider
implications of their influence. He examines Ortega's position
with regard to the Civil War, his ambivalent espousal of socialism,
his emphasis on the importance of the select individual in the
modernisation of society and creation of a *nación vital*; the ap-
propriation of his ideas by Primo de Rivera in the cause of fascism.
He proceeds to give clear explanations of Ortega's philosophical
concerns, such as his criticism of rationalism as a method of enquiry, his belief in the status of each individual human life as
the fundamental reality beyond mind and body, his claims for
perspectivism as a view of the truth transcending both relativism
and absolutism, and his attempt to bring these threads together
to create a new form of philosophical enquiry, the *razón vital*.

This book is intended to be accessible to both Hispanists and
general readers with an interest in literature, history, intellectual
and political thought and philosophy.

José Ortega y Gasset at his house in the calle Monte Esquinza in Madrid.

An Introduction
to the
Politics and Philosophy of
José Ortega y Gasset

ANDREW DOBSON

Department of Politics, University of Keele

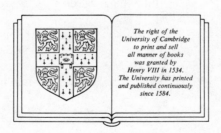

The right of the
University of Cambridge
to print and sell
all manner of books
was granted by
Henry VIII in 1534.
The University has printed
and published continuously
since 1584.

CAMBRIDGE UNIVERSITY PRESS

CAMBRIDGE

NEW YORK   NEW ROCHELLE   MELBOURNE   SYDNEY

Published by the Press Syndicate of the University of Cambridge
The Pitt Building, Trumpington Street, Cambridge CB2 1RP
32 East 57th Street, New York, NY 10022, USA
10 Stamford Road, Oakleigh, Melbourne 3166, Australia

First published 1989

Printed in Great Britain at the University Press, Cambridge

British Library cataloguing in publication data
Dobson, Andrew
An introduction to the politics and the
philosophy of José Ortega y Gasset. –
(Cambridge Iberian and Latin American Studies).
1. Spanish philosophy. Ortega y Gasset, José, 1883–1955
I. Title
196'.1

Library of Congress cataloguing in publication data
Dobson, Andrew
An introduction to the politics and philosophy of José Ortega y
Gasset / Andrew Dobson.
p. cm. – (Cambridge Iberian and Latin American studies)
Bibliography.
Includes index.
ISBN 0–521–36068–4
1. Ortega y Gasset. José, 1883–1955 – Political and social views.
2. Spain – politics and government – 20th century. I. Title
II. Series.
JC271.074D63 1989
320'.01 – dc19 88–20323

ISBN 0 521 36068 4

GG

For my family in England and my family in Spain

Contents

Acknowledgements

I am indebted to the Spanish Government for making available a one-year scholarship to enable me to study in Madrid in 1983–4 – happily coinciding with celebrations for the centenary of Ortega's birth. The continuation of the work I began there was made possible by a Postdoctoral Fellowship awarded by the Economic and Social Research Council, held between 1984 and 1987.

During the writing of this book I have made a number of trips to Spain and have spent much time at the Fundación Ortega y Gasset in Madrid. I would like to take this opportunity to thank everyone there for their help, encouragement and friendliness. I am particularly grateful for permission both to quote from Ortega's private correspondence, held at the Fundación, and to make use of a Fundación archive photograph for the frontispiece.

In Oxford, Professor Ian Michael of the Spanish sub-Faculty was quick to make an 'outsider' feel part of a family of a literary experts, and I am especially indebted to him for unhesitatingly putting sub-Faculty software and hardware at my disposal. The gestation period of this book would have been considerably longer without this facility. Thanks in this context are also due to those at St John's College, Oxford, who accepted me as a member for the three year duration of the ESRC fellowship, and who allowed me generous use of college facilities.

I am profoundly grateful to Leslie Macfarlane, Frances Lannon, Sabina Lovibond, and to my close friends Tom Buchanan, Reg Mills and Frank Rodrigues for reading and suggesting amendments (mostly incorporated) to parts of the typescript. None of them have read it all, so I can safely say that the remaining shortcomings are entirely my responsibility.

Suggestions made by the anonymous readers at Cambridge University Press have resulted in a tighter book than would otherwise have been the case, and I am grateful to them, and to my editor Kevin Taylor, for their sound advice.

The 'invisible hand' behind this book is that of Mary Warnock who has read none of it but who was unfailingly encouraging as I progressed towards the position of being able to write it. In a very real sense the book owes its existence to her unflagging help and enthusiasm.

Likewise, this book could not have been written without Marie Ruiz, of Oxford, and Helena Mazo and Concha Pérez Moreno, of the Stanton School, Madrid. These people helped me to acquire a respectable standard of Spanish in a shorter time than I would ever have believed possible, and if I have damaged Ortega's text in translation then that is my fault, not theirs.

Finally, I should like to thank my colleagues in the Spanish Studies Seminar which ran at Oxford between 1985 and 1987 for listening to paper after interminable paper as I struggled to make Ortega comprehensible to them, and therefore to myself. Using them as a sounding-board surely tried their patience, and I sincerely hope that their informed demands for clarification have a presence in the pages that follow.

Ortega's major works in English translation

*Most recent English language versions
in chronological order of composition*

Meditaciones del Quijote (1914) – *Meditations on Quixote* (Norton, New York, 1984)

Investigaciones psicológicas (1916) – *Psychological Investigations* (Norton, New York/London, 1987)

España invertebrada (1921) – *Invertebrate Spain* (Norton, New York, 1957)

El tema de nuestro tiempo (1923) – *The Modern Theme* (Harper, New York, 1961)

La deshumanización del arte e ideas sobre la novela (1925) – *The Dehumanization of Art and Notes on the Novel* (Princeton University Press, 1972)

The 1968 edition from the same publisher (entitled *The Dehumanization of Art and other essays on art, culture and literature*) also contains 'On the doctrine of the point of view in art', 'Asking for a Goethe from within', and 'The self and other'.

La rebelión de las masas (1929) – *The Revolt of the Masses* (University of Notre Dame Press, Indiana, 1985)

¿Qué es filosofía? (1929) – *What is Philosophy?* (Norton, New York, 1960)

Misión de la universidad (1930) – *Mission of the University* (Princeton University Press, 1962)

Unas lecciones de metafísica (1932–3) – *Some Lessons in Metaphysics* (Norton, New York, 1969)

En torno a Galileo (1933) – *Man and Crisis* (Norton, New York, 1962)

Sobre la razón histórica (1940 and 1944) – *Historical Reason* (Norton, New York/London, 1984)

Estudios sobre el amor (1941) – *On Love* (Meridian, New York, 1960)

Historia como sistema (1941) – *History as a System and other Essays towards a Philosophy of History* (Norton, New York, 1962). Also contains 'The sportive origin of the state', 'Unity and diversity of Europe', and 'Man the technician'.

Pròlogo a 'Veinte años de caza mayor', del Conde de Yebes (1942) – Meditations on Hunting (Charles Scribener's, New York, 1985)

Origen y epílogo de la filosofía (1944–53) – The Origin of Philosophy (Norton, New York, 1967)

La idea del principio de Leibniz y la evolución de la teoría deductiva (1947–8) – The Idea of Principle in Leibniz and the Evolution of Deductive Theory (Norton, New York, 1971)

Una interpretación de la historia universal (1948–9) – An Interpretation of Universal History (Norton, New York, 1975)

El hombre y la gente (1949) – Man and People (Norton, New York, 1963)

Introduction

In the state of Arkansas in the United States of America there is a small town called Humphrey. Sometime in 1951 a woman in Humphrey called Joan Harlan gave birth to a son, and set about finding a godfather for him. Two years before, in July 1949, a Spaniard called José Ortega y Gasset – described somewhat uncertainly by *Time* magazine as a 'Philosopher – Teacher – Statesman' – and Albert Schweitzer, the medical missionary, had spent a fortnight in Aspen, Colorado, as the main attractions at a conference on the occasion of Goethe's bicentennial celebrations. *Time* quoted the conference's organiser, Robert Hutchins of the University of Chicago, as saying that the theme of the conference was to call attention to a 'consciousness of moral responsibilities, liberty and the dignity of man'. In the context of the post-war world when the incarcerations and the carnage of 1939–45 were still fresh in the memory this enterprise was newsworthy, and *Newsweek* as well as *Time* sent reporters to the event. It is possible that Joan Harlan of Humphrey, Arkansas, first read of Ortega in one of these magazines in July 1949, or at least that she became aware of him through the publicity generated by his visit to Aspen and the things he said there. In any event, she clearly found him an attractive figure because two years later she wrote to Ortega in Spain asking him to be the godfather of her new-born son. Ortega replied as follows: 'I don't really know what use my being a godfather to your son is going to be, but your wish aroused a great feeling of warmth in me and so you can count on my acceptance. Oh yes – and give a kiss to the happy little Ortega Harlan' (FOG C. 208 JK 48/114 3.1.52).[1]

---

[1] The key for letters is given at the end of the bibliography. All translations of Ortega's work are my own.

1

It is tempting to suggest that only a figure of some international renown would find him- or herself being asked to be the godfather of a child from half-way around the world. Joan Harlan's request was certainly not the product of an idiosyncratic taste for someone whom we might now consider to be an obscure Spanish essayist, but rather of her admiration for a man who had the highest of profiles in the Western world from the 1930s to the 1950s. That he was a figure of great repute in the intellectual and political circles of Spain itself throughout the first half of the century is generally accepted, but it is harder now to recreate the international reputation he had acquired.

In 1943 he wrote to a friend that there had been 'a huge increase in the number of my books sold *throughout the world*, to the point where I am today the most widely-read writer of philosophy in North America, Germany, Hungary, the Scandinavian countries, and am beginning to be so in England and France' (FOG C.204 JK 86/134 15.12.43). Likely as not this is an exaggeration and certainly in the case of England his optimism was unfounded. But the fact that he was even able to suggest it as a possibility may come as a surprise to many students (and not a few teachers) of philosophy for whom Ortega is, at most, a shape without substance. The translation of *La rebelión de las masas*[2] into over a dozen languages secured Ortega an international reputation which he consolidated from 1936 onwards during the years of exile from Spain by visits and lecture tours to most of the countries of Europe, and some outside it. In Germany in particular hundreds of thousands of copies of *La rebelión de las masas* were sold and in the post-war wasteland of that country his lectures were attended by large numbers of people. As he wrote to his friend and disciple Julián Marías in 1951, when 1,300 people came each evening to hear him give four lectures in Munich on the idea of the nation: 'You cannot imagine the tenderness, enthusiasm and kindness which have been showered on me throughout Germany' (FOG C.208 JK 56/114 23.2.52).

Indeed his international profile was such that by 1959, four years after Ortega's death, a reviewer in the *Times Literary Supplement* felt able to say that Ortega had 'earned a secure niche in the European hall of fame' (10 July 1959, p. 414). Ask anyone outside Spain today, however, if they have heard of Ortega, and the answer is likely

---

[2] English translations for titles of major works may be found in the list at the beginning of the book.

be no. If the answer is yes, it will probably be followed by 'But I haven't read anything by him.' I am reminded of a comment by an English friend of mine in Madrid who, on our first meeting, asked me what I was doing in Spain. When I told him that I was preparing a book on Ortega y Gasset he said: 'Hm . . . interesting. Tell me, I've heard of Ortega but who is this Gasset fellow?' In my experience the evidence suggests that Ortega's niche in the European hall of fame was all but secure and it is one of the aims of this introduction to suggest both the reasons for his relative decline and the factors which could lead to his resuscitation.

It should be said that even at the height of his fame he was never particularly well-known or well-received in Britain. He did not visit the country until the summer of 1951 when Glasgow University conferred an honorary doctorate upon him during the celebrations for its 500th anniversary. On that occasion he spent four days in Glasgow and five in London where Alan Pryce-Jones, then editor of the *Times Literary Supplement*, met him and later described him on the BBC's Third Programme as 'a sharp-eyed, talkative, imperious old gentleman, in the incongruous surroundings of a South Kensington house, watching a troupe of Spanish gypsy dancers' (*The Listener*, 22 November 1951, p. 891).

As far as I know, Ortega made just two other visits to Britain – the second of which was in October 1954, just one year before he died. He was invited by a Mr Brown of the British Institute of Management to give a talk in Torquay. He agreed to go but wrote to José Miguel Ruiz Morales of the Spanish Embassy in London that, 'For me this talk is a big nuisance because for some months I have been too ill and too bad-tempered to be bothered with anything, let alone something of so little interest to me (FOG C.210 JK 32/54 14.10.54). He visited Torquay, gave the speech that was required of him and returned home directly. In February 1955 he wrote to a friend that, 'The trip, to England was not of the slightest importance' and said that he had read, with great difficulty, something that he had written many years before (FOG C.211 JK 37/54 8.2.55). Thus ended Ortega's personal acquaintance with Britain.

Even before these visits, his relationship with British readers had not been particularly fruitful. In 1933 he wrote to Federico de Onís that, 'My experience with British publishers has been pretty bad', announced that he had broken with Allen and Unwin and that he had had no success with anyone else (FOG C.203 JK 32/134 19.5.33).

La rebelión de las masas itself was received relatively poorly and in 1934
he was moved to write to a Professor Greenwood, presumably of some
British University, asking him what he thought were the reasons
behind the cool reception given his book. Professor Greenwood's
answer is not extant, but he might have replied that it had something
to do with the different tradition within which Ortega was writing,
particularly with respect to liberalism. The universalist and collectivist traditions which British liberalism acquired as a *sine qua non* of
its survival as a progressive ideology in a market-place increasingly
dominated by socialism, went a long way towards preventing *La rebelión
de las masas* from being required reading for British liberals. The
'supreme-individual' liberalism which Ortega proffered was not acceptable to the hybrid tradition which British liberals had been developing for at least a third of a century. Importantly, this provides a clue
as to the relative popularity of Ortega in the United States: his
liberalism is much closer to the 'meritocratic' or 'frontier-spirit' individualism of American politics than it is to anything in recent British
traditions.

However, even if Ortega enjoyed an uneven reputation in the
Western world in general and in Europe in particular, it is still true
to say that by the time of his death and in the years immediately following, he had 'achieved fame on both sides of the Atlantic' (*Times Literary
Supplement*, 1 March 1957, p. 130). Looked at from the vantage point
of 1987 it is hard to recapture this Ortega, a figure of international
standing, rubbing shoulders with the mightiest and most intelligent
of his time, counting on a large and faithful following and with his books
conspicuously for sale in the bookshops of over thirty countries. The fact
is that in the space of about twenty-five years Ortega, both inside and
outside Spain, has all but disappeared from view and his work and
memory are only preserved by small coteries of interested folk. One of
his disadvantages, in the context of British universities (where foreign
language courses tend to be dominated by the study of literature), is that
he never published any fiction. The ideas of his erstwhile mentor Miguel
de Unamuno, on the other hand, are known to a wider audience in this
country precisely because the Salamancan philosopher wrote work which
can legitimately be studied as 'literature'.

More generally speaking, the reasons for Ortega's decline vary from
country to country. In Italy, Leonardo Sciascia has written of the
popularity of Marx, Lukács and Gramsci which submerged any
tendency there may have been to take Ortega seriously. He comments:

'If Italian culture spent the war years delivered over to the debate between Croce and Gentile, the post-fascist or anti-fascist years were marked and dominated by the Croce-Gramsci debate. There was not much room, then, for an essayist like Ortega' (*El País* supplement, 7 May 1983, p. 13). In France, Albert Camus – 'one of the few French people who read him' – proposed to translate Ortega but never did; Gallimard studiously ignored him, and David Mata refers to the 'obscurantism' and 'provincialism of French intellectual life' as factors which have contributed to Ortega's lack of popularity (*ibid.* pp. 14–15).

By 1936 in Spain itself Ortega's endeavours had led to the appearance of a philosophical school known as the School of Madrid, the members of which will most likely be unfamiliar to an English-speaking readership: Julián Marías, Fernando Vela, Xavier Zubiri, José Gaos, Antonio Rodríguez Huéscar, José Ferrater Mora, Paulino Garagorri and others. This school was extremely influential and productive within Spain and it is possible that without the disruption caused by the Civil War, its influence would have extended to Europe as a whole. As it was, many of the school's members went into exile in America (Gaos to Mexico and Ferrater Mora to Cuba, Chile and finally the United States, for example), and those who stayed in Spain or returned to it at a later date found themselves working in an atmosphere uncongenial to their enterprise. After 1936, says Pedro José Chamizo Domínguez, 'nothing could be the same for philosophy in Spain and never again did a group of such brilliant figures come together to teach in the same place' (1985:156). With the end of the Civil War, teaching was dominated by those acceptable to the Nationalist victors, and the Catholic Church's lack of enthisiasm for Ortega's philosophy (for reasons which will become clear) made its spread highly unlikely. More generally, several of his articles were proscribed during the Franco regime, and Domínguez writes that by the time the ban was lifted in 1969:

Ortega's philosophy was considered by the young to be *démodée*. Times had changed and philosophies of a metaphysical type – among which one would have to include Ortega's – had lost prestige at the same time as historical continuity had been broken. The young Spanish philosophers of the sixties were dazzled by other forms of philosophy, among which Ortega's did not figure. These other types of philosophy were basically of an analytic and neopositivist or Marxist or Nietszchean inspiration. Ortega had become a 'has-been'. Even people like José Ferrater Mora – who remained in sympathy with Ortega's work and about which he wrote an expository book

– set off in a different philosophical direction. Times had changed and
Ortega belonged to a distant past.   (1985: 157)

The situation in which Ortega's philosophy found itself in Spain in
the 1960s has not changed – it still plays only a minor and optional
part in university degree courses. Just what this means is open to interpretation. It may amount to an enlightening comment on Spain's
image of its intellectual self that it all but ignores the achievements
of its greatest twentieth-century philosopher. It may, on the other
hand, be a realistic assessment of Ortega's philosophical worth, or
it may, finally, be an example of how historical figures come and go
– that their importance is not absolute, but relative to the needs of
the moment. I shall not prejudice the rest of the book by passing judgement at this early stage.

There is no doubt, nevertheless, that Ortega's fortune in Spain was
pretty much cast by the Civil War and its consequences. In a battle
in which there are only two sides there is no room for sitting on the
fence. Ortega's very public silence during the Civil War and its aftermath was intended to be an eloquent attempt to express his dissatisfac-
tion with both sides. The danger is that such silence leaves one
defencelessly open to interpretation: if one does not pronounce one's
partiality others will surely do so. The political variety to be found
in Ortega's work left him particularly open to distortion, and even
to fabrication. Opponents of the Nationalists, for example, would con-
centrate on works open to charges of reaction such as *España invertebrada*
and *La rebelión de las masas*, while critics of the Republicans would
find good reason in Ortega's liberalism and non-Catholicism to con-
sign him to the 'reds'.

Under these Manichean conditions balanced opinions are hard to
produce and even less likely to survive. Ortega's death itself was
manipulated by the regime as the newspapers *Ya* and *ABC* reported
that he had 'died a Christian' by taking the last rites just before slip-
ping finally into unconsciousness. It was soon discovered that this was
untrue and it is said that Ortega's actual response to the priests'
offer of a final blessing was, 'Away with these cockroaches!' Again,
after suffering at the hands of the Socialist Party during the Civil War
and its aftermath, Ortega's memory was placed at the service of the
cause by none other than the socialist intellectual, Luis Araquistáin.
Mellowed now, it should be said, since his radical days with the socialist
journal *Leviatán* during the Second Republic, Araquistáin wrote in

December 1955 that Ortega should be defended because, 'to defend him is also to defend the intellectual honour of the free Spain to which he belonged' (*El Socialista*, 1 December 1955).

This utilisation of a personality and his work is no surprise given the political situation engendered by the Civil War and Franco's subsequent dictatorship. I only make the point so as to illustrate the unlikelihood of arriving at a rounded view of a person's work under these conditions: in a battle between good and evil, complexity is not at a premium. It is possible that as the conditions which cut interpretations of Ortega in two recede into the past, more balanced studies of his work – particularly his politics – will be forthcoming. Indeed, it is the purpose of the first half of this present book to provide the stuff of such a study.

Reasons have already been suggested for the ignorance in Britain of Ortega's political and sociological theories, and it is possible that as the post-war collectivist consensus continues to break down, room will once again be found for Ortega in the discourse of political theory: it is likely that the New Right, for example, would find some of his writings sympathetic.

An anecdote may help to make this last assertion more comprehensible. In December 1986 I reviewed Anthony Kerrigan's excellent new translation of Ortega's *La rebelión de las masas* for the *Times Literary Supplement*. A copy of the review found its way to California where it came to the attention of someone who was evidently partial to at least some aspects of Ortega's politics. The person in question wrote me a letter dominated by one enigmatic phrase, typed in red: 'The basis for world freedom has been found!'

Curious, I took up the offer to write for further information, and four weeks later received a second letter in which my correspondent wrote, 'I am delighted to introduce you to the powerful new concepts upon which the survival of our species and the attainment of World Freedom depend.' Enclosed with this letter were five small cards, collectively entitled 'Thrust for Freedom.' Each card had a heading such as 'What is Property?', 'Who stands for Freedom?' and 'Who is a Progressive?', and the common denominator in all of them was an avowal of the claims of individual freedom against any form of collectivism.

A similar theme emerges in a letter from one C. R. Fisher of the Canadian Club of New York, based at the Waldorf – Astoria Hotel. Writing in December 1954, Fisher congratulates Ortega on *La rebelión*

de las masas, which Fisher's club has been discussing, and says: 'Have
you any recent writings that could be published here to help our program, especially with the youth and college students, who come under
the teachings and influence of left-wing and Communist professors,
of which our colleges are full?' (FOG C. 161 JK 80/102 14.12.54).
Ortega's *Rebelión* is firmly within the traditions of North American
meritocratic liberalism and both Fisher and my Californian correspondent obviously picked this up. It is the blanket rejection of
collectivism which lends weight to the contention that, given today's
political – ideological situation, the New Right will probably find him
of more immediate interest than anyone else. I hasten to add, however,
that, as will become clear, such an interpretation would far from
exhaust the content of Ortega's political thought. A New Right use
of Ortega would be as eclectic as any so far made of his political
thought, and there is much in him that would not be of the slightest
benefit to the anti-collectivist consensus.

Be that as it may, the ignorance in Britain of Ortega's thought is
strange if one considers the status he acquired throughout Europe
in the 1940s and 1950s. His philosophy, in particular, constitutes an
almost total blind-spot. There is no reference to him in Bertrand
Russell's *History of Western Philosophy*, none in Frederick Copleston's
History of Philosophy, none in J. O. Urmson's *Concise Encyclopedia of
Western Philosophy and Philosophers*, and none in Antony Flew's *An
Introduction to Western Philosophy*. Even Roger Scruton, who one would
think might find something of interest in Ortega, has no room for
him in his *From Descartes to Wittgenstein: A Short History of Modern
Philosophy*. The only article of any length I have found on Ortega in
a philosophical journal is A. Armstrong's 'Ortega's philosophy' in
The Philosophical Quarterly of April 1952. The article is rambling and
inadequate and contains nothing concrete on Ortega's mature
philosophy – i.e. that developed from approximately 1928 onwards.
Curiously, the best short introduction to Ortega's thought is to be
found in an article entitled 'Ortega y Gasset's philosophy of art' by
Leon Livingstone, mentioned in the bibliography. Livingstone provides a useful summary of Ortega's early work and makes admirably
clear use of the only piece of 'later' work he had to hand: Ortega's
1929–30 lectures entitled *'What is philosophy?'*

One must look at the historical circumstances to make sense of the
lack of popularity of Ortega's philosophy in Britain. J. Waldron has
written in another context of the twentieth century having 'an

atmosphere in philosophy congenial to analysis in general and preoccupied to the point of obsession with analytical rigours and precision' (1985:2). Ortega's philosophy, highly metaphorical and critical of the transportation of mathematical standards of precision to the human sciences, was unlikely to flourish in such conditions. The following anecdote illustrates the gap in philosophical priorities between Spain and Britain into which Ortega's philosophy was likely to disappear. In the mid-1950s Julián Marías, the most prolific living exponent of Ortega's thought, visited Oxford and took part in one of the weekly discussions organised by Gilbert Ryle in Magdalen College. After the event, Marías was asked how it had gone and he is said to have replied, 'They don't think that metaphysics is a proper subject.' This must have seemed particularly peculiar to him given that Ryle, at the time, was the Waynflete Professor of Metaphysical Philosophy. The problem for Ortega's type of philosophy in the British philosophical context was also recognised by Alan Pryce-Jones: 'if A. J. Ayer and Gilbert Ryle are right in propounding that the business of philosophy is to solve puzzles rather than to discover truths, Ortega was [sic] not a philosopher at all' (The Listener, 22 November 1951, p. 891).

The fact is that the circumstances of British philosophy were not congenial to the study of a philosophy such as Ortega's. We might add to this the observation that philosophers in Britain have traditionally been reluctant to look to the continent for inspiration. As Alan Montefiore expresses it:

A generation ago few students (or even professors) of philosophy on either side of the English Channel knew very much about the philosophy that was being produced, studied and debated on the other side. Nor for the most part had they any interest in seeking to find out. Indeed, they felt in general fully justified in their ignorance by a settled conviction of the frivolity, superficiality and lack of any rigorous intellectual value of that of which they were accordingly more than content to remain ignorant.

(Descombes, 1980: vii)

Montefiore is referring specifically to France here, but it is clear that the sentiment applies throughout the continent and particularly, from a British perspective, to Spain. Montefiore then moves to a more optimistic note:

Now – happily – times seem to be changing. On both sides of the same Channel signs are multiplying of a serious desire to learn about what has been and is going on on the other side, and even to participate in it; and, beyond the often still persisting incomprehension, there is an increasing return to the goodwill of mutual recognition and respect. (*ibid.*)

This is most certainly not true of Spanish philosophy and British awareness of it. The 'opening up' of the British philosophical mind to continental stimuli stops at the Pyrenees, behind which it seems to be believed that nothing of interest has been, or could be, produced. It might be argued that nothing of interest *has* been produced by Spanish philosophers, but a precondition for this belief would be at least one book – or even an article – demonstrating that this was so. To my knowledge no such book or article has yet been written.

One further factor ought to be taken into account, I think, in order to explain British reluctance to take Spanish philosophy seriously. The refusal to believe that Spain could produce any useful philosophy is embedded in the wider belief that Spain, with her sand, sea and sun, is a land of trivia, levity and frivolity and not much else. There are obviously a large number of eminent Hispanophiles – generally historians or students of literature – who know much better than this, but their influence on Spain's image in other disciplines has been slight. As far back as 1922, a reviewer for the *Times Literary Supplement* described Spain as the '*cul de sac* of Europe and Africa' (28 October 1922, p. 609), a sentiment which, generally speaking, has survived to this day: the fame of Federico García Lorca, Luis Buñuel, Salvador Dalí and Pablo Picasso is the exception rather than the rule.

The international projection of the qualities of intellectual Spain was certainly not helped by the Franco regime's determination to earn foreign exchange through the exploitation of Spain's tourist potential. The dominant image of Spain for at least two generations of Europeans, and Britons in particular, has been that of the delights of a cheap seaside holiday with national necessities such as hamburgers thoughtfully provided. The rapid growth and spectacular ugliness of resorts such as Benidorm and Torremolinos are a testimony both to tourism's mighty earnings and its potentially corrosive effect on a country's international image. This effect has, I think, been profound. David Bowie may not be the most respectable of academic sources, but his refusal a few years ago to give a concert in Spain because he 'did not want to play in Africa' is illustrative: apart from being offensive to Africa it neatly articulates a generally held British prejudice towards Spain. Academics who consider themselves absolved from such superficiality should ponder the words of another *Times*

Literary Supplement reviewer whose subliminal presumption caused him to write approvingly of Ortega that he 'was not ashamed of being a Spaniard' (10 July 1959, p. 414), as though 'Spanishness' was a condition to which shame was and is most normally and naturally attached.

I would suggest, then, that there are various factors which contribute to Ortega's low profile in Britain. His political perspective has only been attractive to a narrow section of the community and has found no tradition in which to assert itself. His philosophy encounters the same problem of the lack of a tradition, coupled with the additional unwillingness of British philosophy to engage with its continental neighbours. Further, for many people Spain is only reluctantly admitted to be a part of the European continent anyway.

All these factors are, however, historical and therefore open to flux and change, and it is not fanciful to suggest that the conditions which have generated such a stunted perspective of Spanish culture are in the process of modulation. For instance, the government clearly believes – rightly or wrongly – that Spanish membership of the European Economic Community will contribute to a lifting of the veil between Spain and the rest of Europe. If they are right, then European – and particularly British – opinions of Spain may become more respectful. Something, in any case, seems to be happening already, as Britain's Sunday magazines now contain holiday advertisements for a Spain beyond and behind the beaches, and David Bowie finally gave concerts in Spain in the spring of 1987.

As far as Ortega himself is concerned, continental philosophy *is* becoming a respectable issue to pursue in British universities, and it is possible that the interest shown in philosophies from France and Germany will open a door through which someone may be willing and able to coax him. Finally, from a political perspective, it has already been suggested that the demise of the collectivist consensus and the associated rise of the 'meritocratic' liberalism which has taken a grip on both sides of the Atlantic, may provide more fertile ground for a reading of Ortega's own brand of liberalism. It is to this changing cultural context that the present book belongs.

Chapter 1 offers some reflections on the context of Ortega's political life and the principal intellectual influences upon him. Chapters 2–6 comprise a discussion of Ortega's political thought through a sustained consideration of his relationship with various political ideologies and concepts such as socialism and liberalism, elitism and democracy. Generally speaking, very little political-theoretical work has been done on the Spanish intellectuals who were politically engaged during the period under discussion. Phrases such as 'Unamuno's socialist phase' and 'Ortega's liberal years' are tossed around with little attention to ideological detail, and this section of the present book seeks to impose some analytical rigour on the material. I have not attempted to define the ideologies and concepts under consideration (what is socialism?, what is democracy?) – a task impossible to complete to everyone's satisfaction in the limited space available. I can only hope that the beliefs and notions pinpointed are generally recognised as being important to the ideology or concept in question.

Interpretations of Ortega's political perspective are notoriously wide-ranging: in the *Revista de Historia Militar* (No. 55, 1983), for example, Colonel José María Garate Córdoba refers to him as a 'thinker of the left', while Susan Sontag has categorised his political opinions as 'horrible', 'detestable' and 'reactionary' (*Triunfo*, 19 September 1970). The conclusion is reached in this book that Ortega fits no general label but that he comes closest to a species of select-individual, meritocratic liberalism. The typical claim that he moved from liberalism to conservatism is decisively rejected in favour of the view that tensions which arose early in his career were maintained throughout, and that he never decisively abandoned any one of a complex variety of political perspectives. Ortega is presented as a representative of liberal thought in a time of crisis for liberalism in general and in Spain in particular. No bourgeois revolution had ever occurred in Spain and although the historical conditions in which it might have been produced had at last arrived, so had opposition to it in the form of a nascent industrial proletariat on the one hand, and various corporatist solutions to the difficulties of international finance and national grievances, on the other. Finding himself on this historical fault-line Ortega moved around the ideological market seeking the means of achieving what he considered to be the ultimate goal: the creation of a modern Spain, fit to take its place among the most advanced of European nations.

Ortega's philosophical career was even longer than his public political career and adequate coverage of the development of his philosophy would require a book in its own right. Not wanting to risk a superficial treatment, I have chosen (in chapters 7–10) to deal only with his mature thought, and then only with its basis. Discussion focuses on Ortega's search for the answer to what he considered to be the basic question of metaphysics: what constitutes the universe's *realidad radical* or 'radical reality'? His answer, the reasons he gives for it, and the implications of his answer are considered in the context of his view of the nature of truth and of 'objects'. Finally, his notion of *razón vital*[3] or 'reason from life's point of view' is unpacked for inspection.

Ortega's university course of 1929–30 is represented for the purposes of this book as announcing the beginning of his mature philosophy, a philosophy whose parameters are generally marked by the following figures: Friedrich Nietzsche, Henri Bergson and, particularly, Edmund Husserl, Wilhelm Dilthey and Martin Heidegger. I suggest at the beginning of chapter 7 that the publication of Heidegger's *Sein und Zeit* was the catalyst for Ortega's concentrated attempt to organise his philosophy, and it is the post-*Sein und Zeit* period with which this part is primarily concerned.

This book is not the place for an exploration of the precise philosophical relationship between Ortega and Heidegger, although it is one of the most interesting possibilities thrown up by a knowledge of the former's thought. The accepted history of philosophy would have it that Heidegger was the first 'Heideggerian', but Ortega argues that his own similar ideas predated Heidegger's by some thirteen or fourteen years (*Obras completas*, vol. 8, p. 275).[4] In Spain itself there is considerable disagreement over Ortega's claim, with Julián Marías, for instance, arguing in his favour, and José Luis Molinuevo protesting Heidegger's originality. The present book aims to provide the basis for discussion of the issue by non-Spanish-speaking reader. Ortega and Heidegger, in any case, knew each other personally and maintained an amicable relationship – Ortega possessed a Spanish translation of *Sein und Zeit* which Heidegger had dedicated to him 'with friendly greetings'.

Husserl and Heidegger – just two of the philosophers with and against whom Ortega considered himself to be thinking – are both respectable members of the cast of characters of twentieth-century philosophy. The second half of this book is intended, in sum, to introduce the philosophy of Ortega and thus to help non-Spanish speakers come to their own decision as to whether or not he deserves a higher profile in the modern history of Western philosophy than he has hitherto been accorded.

Ortega was an extraordinarily prolific writer on a dauntingly wide

---

[3] Ortega's concept has invariably been translated as 'vital reason'. I believe this to be an inadequate rendering and my reasons for adopting a different approach are given in chapter 10.

[4] Hereafter, references to Ortega's complete works will take the following form: (OC 8, 275).

range of subjects and this book does not pretend to cover them all. The topics with which it does deal, however – his metaphysics and his politics – provide the indispensable foundations on which other notions are constructed and on which they depend. His ideas on the novel, his aesthetics and his theories on education, for example, are only intelligible on the basis of an understanding of the themes covered here. To this extent these pages comprise not only an introduction to his politics and philosophy, but also to the richness and variety of the whole of his prodigious and erudite contribution to the history of Western thought.

I

1

History, politics and biography

In 1883, the same year in which Marx and Wagner died and Keynes and Mussolini were born, Dolores Gasset y Artime, of Madrid, gave birth to her second child, a boy, and called him José.

The young José Ortega y Gasset lived in an immensely busy household, for his father, besides being editor of *El Imparcial's* prestigious literary supplement *El Lunes*, was also a deputy in the Cortes for Padrón (Galicia). From a very early age he would have had contact with a wide range of literary and political characters through his father's daily *tertulias*.[1] His childhood was materially comfortable. His oft-quoted remark of later years that he was 'born on a rotary press' is itself significant of the relative wealth into which he was born: most newspapers simply could not afford one.

By 1887, aged four, Ortega was beginning to read, and in 1890 he won a toy horse from his parents for memorising the first chapter of *Don Quijote* – this in a country whose illiteracy rate was 71.6 per cent. Spanish illiteracy rates were, in a Northern European context, very high, and they remained so for a long time. Even in 1930 44 per cent of the population could neither read nor write (Martínez Cuadrado, 1983: 124). This factor is, I think, of considerable political importance, especially in the context of would-be modernisers (like Ortega) of Spanish society. Literacy both helps to define a 'modern society' and is one of the basic requirements for survival in it. The surprise, then, is that so little attention was paid to it by those seeking to model Spain on her Northern European neighbours.

Due to the influence of his mother in September 1891 Ortega and his elder brother Eduardo were enrolled in the Jesuit school of San

---

[1] Informal, regular meeting of friends and acquaintances often held in a café, to discuss issues of intellectual interest.

17

Estanislao de Kostka in Miraflores del Palo, Málaga, where Ortega was
to stay until 1897. Ortega's later recollections of his time in the Jesuit
school were not favourable. Writing a commentary in 1910 on his friend
Ramón Pérez de Ayala's book *AMDG (Ad Majorem Gloriam Dei*, or 'To
the greater glory of God' – the motto of the Jesuits) he talks of 'sadness
and pain' and the offence he felt at what he described as the Jesuit's self-
righteousness and intellectual ignorance (OC 1, 525). Indeed, the recurring theme of Ortega's resentment of the Jesuits is that of his despair at
their intellectual poverty. In 1908 he was to write, in a more general comment on the ideas advanced in the name of the Church, that 'The first
enemies that socialism finds among us are the ignorance of the citizen
and the cunning of the priest. The latter works fruitfully on the former
and seeks to perpetuate it' (OC 10, 87).

Regeneration and reform

There is no doubt that Ortega's experience in Málaga informed his later
sense of the need for a rationalist and secular education in the drive
towards Spain's cultural – and hence, from his perspective, political
– revival. He was not, however, the first to suggest such an enterprise
– indeed, its context had been provided before Ortega was born. In 1876
Giner de los Ríos, recently removed from official academic life by
Cánovas and later to be the subject of great admiration on the part of
Ortega (OC 10, 140), set up the Institución Libre de Ensenanza (ILE)
or Free Institute of Learning. The Institute stressed the free development of personal talents and the education of the 'whole person': students
were not taught 'things', but rather to think for themselves. Participation was held to be more important than examinations and a general
rather than a specific education was given. This tiny institution and its
ideas had a tremendous effect on those who nurtured cultural solutions
to Spain's political problems, although its general social impact was slight
and was essentially confined to reforming elements in the liberal and progressive middle-classes.

Most notable among such elements immediately prior to Ortega
was the collection of individuals, championed by Joaquín Costa,
who came to be known as the regenerationists. Costa, who influenced
Ortega greatly (OC 10, 171–5), was an impassioned opponent of the
oligarchic and *caciquil*[2] nature of the Restoration regime. His four-

---

[2] Adjective from *cacique*: a figure who uses his wealth and/or influence to dominate the
political and administrative life of a village and its surroundings.

point programme for change involved secular education, more efficient industrial production, municipal autonomy and judicial independence – all to be brought about through an interim period of 'iron surgery'.

Costa's practical, rationalist approach to politics had its intellectual analogue in Krausism – a form of thought which was to have great repercussions among those of Ortega's liberalising generation, particularly in the field of education. What Krausism, imported from Germany by Julián Sanz del Río in 1843, brought to Spain was a belief in the power of reason and in the ability of human beings to achieve full self-realisation through its use. According to Karl Christian Friedrich Krause (1781–1832), faults lie not with the world but with the individual who refuses to live by rational precepts. In a practical sense, Krausism provided for a 'reforming and humanitarian impulse', and because of its belief in the linear progress of society and its confidence in reason and the perfectibility of human beings, Krausism represented a philosophy of liberalism in that reason – upon which we are held to depend for our salvation – cannot be exercised freely amid political repression.

The Generation of 1898

In contrast, the political thought of what was essentially a cultural phenomenon – the Generation of 1898 – was influenced by their reaction against rationalism and positivism, and in this way Ortega found himself at the confluence of two distinct modes of thought, one from Europe and one from Spain. Miguel de Unamuno, the most philosophically influential of the Generation of 1898, wrote that: 'Hegel made famous his aphorism that all that is rational is real and all that is real is rational. But there are many of us who, not convinced by Hegel, carry on believing that the real, the really real, is irrational, and that reason is built upon irrationalities' (1973:10). Such thinking led the members of the Generation of 1898 to believe that Spain's political problems were neither exclusively 'rational' in themselves, nor entirely susceptible to rational or analytic treatment. They proposed an almost mystical interpretation and treatment of the Spanish situation. Azorín's *alma* (soul), Maeztu's *raza* (race) and Unamuno's *intrahistoria* (intrahistory) were all attempts to define an essential *hispanidad* (Spanishness) which had to be the starting-point for an understanding of Spain's historical problems. The 1898

Generation was the generation prior to Ortega's and thus provided his immediate Spanish intellectual context. Unamuno, in particular, was a lifelong influence on Ortega's work. Without prejudicing what is to be said in the second half of this book, it is fair to say now that the fact that the description of Ortega's mature philosophy – *razón vital* – is couched in terms derived explicitly from the Salamancan philosopher is evidence of his enduring influence on Ortega's thought.

The refusal of the Generation of 1898 to take Spain's objective historical situation into account has led David Ruiz to call their political analysis 'primitive' (Gabriel Tortella Casares *et al.*, 1981:475). It should be said, too, that this lack of a grip on concrete historical circumstance was a general malaise of the Spanish reforming intelligentsia right up until the Second Republic. Importantly, from the point of view of contextualising Ortega, the political failure of the Generation of 1898 can be seen as the failure of a class. As men of middle-class commercial, rural property and professional backgrounds, they were representative of the inability of the *petit-bourgeoisie*, squeezed between an increasingly organised working-class and the ruling oligarchy, ever to get a hold on power. They had never had their historical moment and by the time their opportunity came, as Spain struggled through the first stages of industrial development, they found themselves confronted by a still-powerful aristocracy and a labour movement whose growth rate was, in European terms, impressive. This was the ailing class in which Ortega found himself.

Taken together, Krausism and the anti-rationalism of the Generation of 1898 constitute the basic and conflicting intellectual context into which Ortega was born. Beyond the differing epistemologies and metaphysics which these two movements represented, they translated, too, into a question about the identity of Spain itself. How far was it to take on the trappings of Europe? How far could it remain intellectually self-sufficient? From this perspective, Ortega's life's work can be seen as an attempt to Hispanicise the European, and Europeanise the Hispanic, and it was precisely this project which was to bring him into open conflict with Unamuno. In 1909 a private letter from Unamuno to Azorín found its way into the newspaper *ABC*. In this letter, Unamuno referred to 'the suckers' who are bewitched by 'those Europeans'. Ortega replied: 'I am, fully and unreservedly, one of those suckers: since I began writing for the public I have hardly written a single page in which the word Europe does not appear with symbolic aggression. For me, all Spain's afflictions begin and end with this word' (OC 1, 128). From this point on, the relationship between Unamuno and Ortega went from bad to worse, and although kinder words were sometimes exchanged, as in 1914 when Unamuno was dismissed from his University chair and Ortega defended him, they never recovered the mutual admiration which characterised their earlier dealings.

Germany and France

At the turn of the century, despite the best efforts of Sanz del Río, who had lectured on Kant, Fichte, Schelling and Hegel, as well as Krause, German intellectual influence on Spain was slight. Indeed, Sanz was distressed that no one took the time to learn German so that they could check his version of German idealism with the original. It is significant of the continuing influence of French culture on Spain, rather than German, that Sanz's students had to corroborate his remarks with French translations of the German philosophers. It is not surprising, then, that an early influence on Ortega should have been Ernest Renan (1823–92) rather than, say, Schelling. Ortega once said of Renan that 'his books have been with me ever since I was a child' (OC 1, 438), and the similarities between the two men are remarkable. Renan's belief that reason and knowledge provided the key to health and virtue, his renunciation of Catholicism, his early defence of Saint-Simonian socialism, his desire to see society reorganised around elites, and his later criticism of democracy as a directionless popular will, all have their echoes in Ortega's life and work.

In the midst of the predominantly French influences of Ortega's early period, his German studies had basically been confined to readings of Nietzsche undertaken in his late teens with his friend Ramiro de Maeztu – readings soon consigned to a youthful test-bed of ideas, experimented upon but not thought worthy of incorporation into production (OC 1, 91–5). But in February 1905, as Spain was about to enter its second year of terrible drought, Ortega made the first of two early visits to Germany which were both to change his life and leave an enduring mark on Spanish intellectual history.

To Germany

Why did he go? I think it a mistake to say, as most commentators do, that he went to Germany because he had a specific philosophical mission in mind. This would have needed a clearly defined understanding of what was available in Germany – an understanding Ortega simply did not have. Indeed, in a letter to Francisco Navarro Ledesma of 9 August 1905 Ortega shows himself at a loss as to what to do with his life, proffering linguistics, philosophy and even editor of *El Imparcial* as possibilities (*Epistolario*, 1974:57).

Ortega studied in Leipzig from April until November 1905. He knew no German when he arrived and experienced great frustration as a result: 'Without knowing the language one is like a new-born babe. One loses the most basically necessary self-confidence and one's ideas are either non-existent or infantile' (*Epistolario*, 1974:17). In the same letter he refers to a deep sense of loneliness and says, 'I haven't cried yet but I haven't been far off it' (p. 12). He found everything to be different and difficult – opening and shutting doors, asking for coffee, catching the tram and sleeping with duvets instead of sheets and blankets. In short, his letters of this period reveal a profound sense of disorientation. By May he is complaining to his friend Navarro Ledesma of three months of almost total solitude and continuing problems with the language. Navarro Ledesma and Ortega Munilla both encourage Ortega to make friends and he replies, somewhat testily, that it is not that easy. In the autumn of 1905 Ortega moved to Berlin in search of a better library and attended the lectures of Georg Simmel who had just published books on Nietzsche and Schopenhauer. He remained in Berlin until the spring of 1906 when he returned to Spain.

In June 1906 Ortega returned to Berlin, courtesy of a scholarship, and on 17 November he enrolled at the University of Marburg. By now he had a clearer motive for being in Germany and this sense of purpose made his second journey more significant than the first. Marburg, thanks largely to the influence of Hermann Cohen (1842–1918), had been Germany's most influential neo-Kantian school since the 1890s. Such was the success of this school in defending the Kantian position against opposition provided by, for example, positivists, German idealists and philosophies such as that of Wilhelm Dilthey, that, as Philip Silver writes:

Until the end of the Great War of 1914, when the 'rationalist optimism' of Marburg, together with that of the rest of the world, received such a brutal blow, movements in philosophy with which we are more familiarised today such as philosophies of 'life', the resurgence of philosophical romanticism, the mysticism of Heidegger etc. were not possible.   (Silver, 1978:63)

Although submerged in the rationalism of Kant in this period, it is curious to note that the work which Ortega produced immediately after his return from Germany – *Renan* (1909) and *Adán en el paraíso* (1910) – cannot be called neo-Kantian in any meaningful sense of the term. Indeed, he did not write anything of any length on Kant until 1921. Without wishing to compromise our view of Ortega's philosophy with a too-hasty early judgement, I believe it safe to say that Ortega did not take a philosophy from Germany, but rather a sense of rigour, a language, and a belief that Spain's political recovery would be dependent upon the putting to use of European culture in a Spanish context. His philosophy, indeed, was to be of just the type (a philosophy of 'life') which Silver would have considered to be impossible in the shadow of Marburg. In 1934 Ortega wrote the following measured and, I think, accurate assessment of the influence of Marburg upon him:

The young people who learned the art of philosophical warfare in the citadel of neo-Kantianism between 1907 and 1911 were no longer neo-Kantian by the time they were twenty-six years old – an age which is usually decisive in the vital course (*carrera vital*) of a thinker's life. We had not, however, completely wasted our time. We had studied Kant profoundly, which is not to be sniffed at. It is more common than is generally believed to come across certain philosophers who spend their whole lives dragging around an inadequate knowledge of Kant like a ball and chain. One cannot compensate for this deficiency because with Kant, European thought turned through 180 degrees and faced up to the past in the spirit of a bold paradox.
(OC 8, 32–3)

As well as contributing to the philosophy seminars of Cohen, to whom he was to refer in 1909 as 'perhaps the greatest living philosopher' (OC 10, 117), Ortega also attended the General Psychology and Pedagogy lectures of Paul Natorp (1854–1924). The influence of Natorp's theory of civic pedagogy on Ortega was to be much more immediate than that of Cohen's neo-Kantianism – his first forays into public life on his return to Spain centred on the potential of education as a weapon of political reform.

Natorp lectured principally on the theories of Pestalozzi – 'a pedagogic genius' according to Ortega (OC 1, 506) – who believed that the ideals of the French Revolution would be best made concrete through the education of character and the deliberate transformation of social characteristics. This coincided with Natorp's position that a community's quality of life 'depended on the civic character of its members' (McClintock, 1968:55) and that, consequently, improvements in the community were realisable through civic education. Ortega, brought up in the context of the Krausist-inspired ILE and nourished on the kind of politics it represented, would have found Natorp's lectures highly relevant.

Back in Spain, Ortega wrote to Francisco Giner on 6 April 1910 that, 'Tomorrow, Thursday, I get married: so the possibility of me being a Don Juan – which I haven't been – perishes' (FOG C/177 JK 53/99). The following day, he and Rosa Spottorno – whom he had met while finishing his doctoral thesis in 1904–5 – were married in Rosa's parents' private chapel in a house on the Plaza Colón where the Torres de Jeréz now stand. The service took the form of a rite for the marriage of believers and non-believers to make room for Ortega's decided non-Catholicism. Rosa, it seems, was as religiously devoted as Ortega's mother. On 25 November, at the precociously early age of twenty-eight, Ortega became Professor of Metaphysics at the University of Madrid on the death of Nicolás Salmerón. He was not to begin teaching there, however, until the beginning of 1912, for in January 1911 he and Rosa went (Ortega's third trip) to Germany (Marburg) where they stayed until October and where their first son, Miguel, was born.

Education and politics

Throughout this period, Ortega had been developing a theory of social change based on education. The impact made by his adolescent contact with both Krausist-influenced thinkers and the ILE itself, through his father's acquaintances, had been reinforced by exposure to the theories of Paul Natorp in Germany in 1906–7. Natorp's belief that changes in community life were realisable through education is clearly echoed in Ortega's lecture given in Bilbao in March 1910, *La pedagogía social como programa político* (Social pedagogy as a political programme); and the idea that political change had to be both prefaced and accompanied by education led, in October 1913, to the founding of the Liga de educación política (League for Political Education) among whose members were Manuel Azaña, Américo Castro, Antonio Machado, Ramiro de Maeztu, and Ramón Pérez de Ayala. In theory the League was neutral as far as party politics were concerned, although Ortega did write that, 'Our association sees great hope in the founding of the Reformist Republican Party, in whose voice it believes it finds an echo of its own aspirations' (OC 10, 249). This assertion was left out of the manifesto that was finally made public, but it gives some idea of the movement away from the Socialist Party that Ortega had made since 1910. By June 1915, however, he had completely parted company with the Reformist Party, commenting that its *rapprochement* with the Liberal Party . . . diverted the trajectory and meaning of this new political association' (OC 10, 316).

The brief that the League gave itself was founded on Ortega's belief that Spain's problem was not simply a problem of culture but of *alta cultura* (advanced culture). By this he meant that Spain suffered from a lack of science, a science whose distinguishing features were first, the inductive method and second, definition. At no stage did the League tackle the problem of how this kind of culture was to be transmitted to the people who inhabited the 'small towns and hamlets' into which they were to go (OC 1, 277), or even whether it was the sort of education they required. If Ortega and his supporters had merely intended raising the cultural consciousness of a select minority, then enterprises such as the Liga de educación política would have been ideal. But the brief was wider than that – Ortega intended no less than the renewal of the whole of Spanish social, political and economic life. In 1910, though, 60 per cent of the Spanish population were still unable to read or write, and one might be forgiven for thinking that the best assault the League could have mounted on Spain's 'cultural problem' was some form of literacy programme. Indeed, Ortega promised that members of the League would first go and listen to those in the countryside whom they would later lead (OC 10, 286), and that the League's brief was to 'investigate the reality of the life of the country' (OC 10, 300). It appears, however, that neither of these options was seriously pursued.

Of course, Ortega's developing belief in the central role of elites in the progress of society encouraged him to propose 'trickle-down' theories of which the League is a perfect practical example. The notion that a cultured minority will eventually transmit their culture downward to the rest of society would have prevented Ortega from conceiving of a broad-based literacy component (for example) in Spain's political/cultural problem. It might be argued, however, that even if the League had attempted to initiate a literacy campaign, it would have foundered. Large-scale successful campaigns of this type generally follow substantial socio-political realignment of a kind which Spain was clearly not experiencing. In any event the League made very little impact on Spanish cultural life at any level and by 1915 it was disbanded.

By 1914, Ortega's political opinions had achieved some sort of coherence and on 23 March of that year, he gave a conference whose title *Vieja y nueva política* (Old and new politics) was to provide the framework for much subsequent discussion in Spain. The speech amounted to a scathing attack on the 'old politics' of Cánovas and his system, which Ortega characterised as inert, lacking in energy and empty of ideas. This is 'official Spain', described as, 'the immense giddy skeleton of an organism which has vanished, which stands up only by virtue of the equilibrium of its bulk, in the same way as they say elephants stay standing up after they die' (OC 1, 272). Political parties had lost touch with the nation, involved in their own game of power-sharing and vote-buying, a game in which entire cemeteries often miraculously rose from the dead to make their way to doctored polling booths on election day. The reservoir of ideas and energy which comprised the rest of the Spanish people was not being tapped. A precondition for a healthy society, continues Ortega, is a government which encourages vitality – something which the Restoration regime was signally failing to do.

The men and women whom Ortega sees as helping release the potential of the Spanish people are clearly defined: 'I am not now speaking to the masses; I address myself to the new privileged men of this unjust society – to doctors and engineers, teachers and businessmen, industrialists and technologists. I address myself to them and I seek their help' (OC 1, 286). In appealing to the professional middle classes, Ortega also asked that they refuse to invent solutions to Spain's problems. A continuing theme of his thought is that political prescriptions should be drawn up in the light of what is politically possible, and that what is politically possible is largely defined by what already, politically, is. From this maxim he derives the following approach to the monarchy/republic debate: 'We begin to work in Spain as we find it. We are monarchists, not so much because we insist on being so, but because it – Spain – is a monarchy' (OC 1, 290). And then: 'If you want a formula – perhaps rough and ready – but the only one which we judge to be dignified, serious and patriotic – with which to express our position, we would say that we are going to act politically as disloyal monarchists' (OC 1, 292).

'Old and new politics', with Ortega still only thirty-one years old but making a large impact on public life, defined his sharpening political perspective – a resolute opposition to the Canovite system; a concern for the future of Spain and a belief in the qualities of the Spanish people which led him to put the health of the country ahead of support for any particular party or form of government; a suspicion of abstract or utopian solutions; the need for a programme of education run by a middle-class elite, and Europe as a model (but only a model) for the revival of Spanish culture. Within three months that Europe was to be plunged into the bloodiest war it had ever known.

Ortega's written contribution to the War was small. In 1915 he wrote, 'The War has lasted a year, and I think I can count myself among those writers who have written least about it' (OC 10, 337). The reason he gives is that words have no place in a war of weapons. He does, however, feel obliged to say something about it because of the way he has been represented in the German and Belgian press – as a Germanophobe and a Germanophile respectively. Given the self-admitted debt which he owed to Germany and its teachers, Ortega was in a difficult position. He surmounted the problem by identifying two Germanies, one political and one cultural. At the political level he said that he preferred England's 'individualist democracy' to the 'statist democracy' of Germany and concluded, 'I agree with those who fervently wish for an allied victory' (OC 10, 340).

Generally speaking, he saw the taking of sides as a painful, but happily transitory, necessity (OC 10, 343). From time to time, though, he suggested that participation in the War would have done Spain more good than remaining neutral. In January 1915 he glanced somewhat enviously at Italy's likely entrance into the War, hinting that Spain, too, ought really not to miss out on an event that was dominating the world stage (OC 10, 274). Certainly towards the end of the War, amid the chaos of 1917 and 1918 in Spain, he remarked that participation might have had a purifying effect, acting like a pair of 'secateurs' on the dead wood of Spanish politics (OC 10, 391).

Publications

Ortega's relatively small output on the First World War coincided with what might best be described as the beginning of a shift in emphasis from politics to publications. In January 1915 he initiated what Jean Michel Desvois has described as 'one of the most important events in the Spanish press in the first part of the century' (1977:72) – the founding of the magazine *España*. Throughout 1915 the magazine moved further to the left and Ortega relinquished editorial control, to be replaced by Luis Araquistáin. In 1922 Manuel Azaña took over, but *España* suffered during the dictatorship of General Miguel Primo de Rivera and ceased publication in 1924.

The year after leaving *España*, Ortega founded *El Espectador* (The Spectator), an enterprise to which he was the only contributor and which was entirely financed by 3,000 private subscriptions. He was to continue producing *El Espectador* until 1934 by which time it numbered eight volumes which now comprises volume 2 of his Complete Works.

As the name suggests, the journal was an attempt to stand back from politics: '*El Espectador* has...a primary intention: to raise a redoubt against politics for me and for those who share my desire for pure vision and pure theory' (OC 2, 17). His explicit reason for this distancing from politics is that it does not deal in truth. Politics, he says, judges ideas by their utility rather than by their truth-content. Politics has its place, but it is a 'secondary spiritual activity' (OC 2, 16) which, by converting truth into utility, deals in lies. 'The political empire', he says, 'is the empire of the lie.'

The pages of *El Espectador* are a fruitful source indeed for those who want to follow the development of Ortega's philosophy. Julián Marías looks at it like this: 'The enterprise called *El Espectador* was not something different from his philosophy; on the contrary, it was its setting in motion – the genuine and effective exercise of that philosophy of which he was beginning to take possession' (Marías, 1983:66).

Ortega's next major involvement in publishing was prompted by the demise of the Gasset family's newspaper, *El Imparcial*. By 1916 the paper had lost much of its prestige and was in a precarious financial situation. Shortly before, the powerful paper manufacturer Nicolás María de Urgoiti had, in his search for a newspaper which would extend the influence of his company La Papelera into the lucrative press market as well as act as a vehicle for the ideas of modernising bourgeois interests, tried in vain to buy *ABC*. The crisis at *El Imparcial* prompted Ricardo Gasset (grandson of the founder) to approach Urgoiti for financial help.

The upshot was that Urgoiti signed a contract by which he would gain control of the paper, and he began to institute reforms. The Gassets did not take kindly to the turn that things were taking, and Urgoiti (with Ortega) found himself increasingly isolated from the aims of the old owners. The crunch came in June 1917 when *El Imparcial* published Ortega's famous article 'Bajo el arco en ruina' ('Beneath the ruined arch'), in which the demanded the recall of the Cortes and criticised the monarchy.

Rafael Gasset (son of the founder) could take no more, and as Urgoiti's contract had not yet been legalised, he – Urgoiti – was removed. A large number of the paper's journalists – Ortega included – went with him.

At this point, Urgoiti decided to set up his own newspaper, *El Sol*, with modern machinery and experienced correspondents who were intended to guarantee its status as a 'quality' newspaper – there were no bullfight reports and no lottery results. The paper included daily supplements on the social sciences, education, medicine, etc., and it cost 10 céntimos – double the normal price. This was a modern bourgeois paper for a modern bourgeoisie – a propaganda vehicle through whose pages (almost exclusively) Ortega was tirelessly to propose the conversion of Spain into a 'modern society' (OC 10, 453).

Urgoiti's programme for *El Sol* shows the similarity between his political prescription and that of Ortega:

Socially, the newspaper will follow with absolute thoroughness those solutions which will lead to greater harmony between labour and capital – an essential base for public peace. Its entire campaign will be against violent demonstrations by workers against sabotages, and against movements in which the proletariat is used as the blind instrument of dangerous stratagems and general strikes, and whose characteristic, so clearly observed in all countries, is fundamentally alien to legitimate workers' demands. At the same time, it ought to inculcate in the capitalist class the basic idea that an obvious sign of progress is the gradual extension of well-being to the greatest possible number of human beings. Equality before the law is not enough: our aim should be to create the possibility of obtaining the necessary means to achieve the general education and specialised instruction which would best suit individual intelligence and temperament.

(quoted in Elorza, 1984:103)

Elorza's own statement of Urgoiti's view makes it clear why the collaboration between him and Ortega was to be so fruitful and long-standing: 'Urgoiti's political intentions consisted in the articulation of a conglomeration of progressive social groups, from a reforming industrial bourgeoisie to a proletariat convinced of the need to follow the road towards improved conditions through contracts and increased productivity (1984:101).

Primo de Rivera

Between 1918 and 1920 (the *trienio bolchevique*, or 'three-year Bolshevik period') this 'articulation' seemed most unlikely. A wave of revolutionary agitation swept through Andalucía, the membership of the syndicalist trade union, the CNT, grew enormously, and Barcelona was the focus of severe labour unrest. On 12 September 1923 the Captain General of Barcelona, Miguel Primo de Rivera, presented a manifesto in the name of restoring public order, finishing the war in Morocco, and putting an end to political corruption. The King accepted Primo's *pronunciamiento* and put him at the head of a military *junta*. In quick time, Primo dissolved the Cortes, suspended the Constitution, abolished the jury system, dissolved town councils and closed down the Ateneo.[3]

In common with most of the rest of the country (but unlike Unamuno) Ortega's reaction to the dictatorship was initially favourable. He agreed with Primo's attack on the 'old politics', and expressed the belief that the dictatorship would have the beneficial effects of a 'short, sharp shock' on the Spanish body politic : 'I think that this passage through dictatorship will amount to an admirable learning experience for today's societies' (OC 11, 35). He also took the opportunity to say that the dictatorship was the perfect expression of public opinion, in the sense that a people gets the government it deserves.

If Ortega appeared unconcerned at the illiberal turn which events were taking, he had, in any case, embarked upon a period of philosophical contemplation and intellectual dissemination whose content was unlikely to be hindered by them. In 1922 he began a series entitled *Biblioteca de ideas del siglo veinte* (Library of Twentieth-Century Ideas), intended to make the very latest European ideas available to the Spanish reader. A curtailed list of authors illustrates Ortega's belief that Germany was still Europe's intellectual centre of gravity: Oswald Spengler, the physicist Max Born, and the biologist Von Uexkull.

[3] Cultural centre – in this case in Madrid – usually patronised by the intellectual elite.

In July 1923 the first issue of what was to be Ortega's longest-running (it still thrives today) and most famous project appeared: the *Revista de Occidente*. The quality of contributors was high – Alberti, Baroja, Lorca, Pérez de Ayala, for example. Articles by renowned European thinkers were translated – Brentano, Fichte, Hegel, Heimsoeth, Husserl, Kierkegaard, Russell, Scheler, Simmel, Jung, Freud and so on. The print run was 3,000 copies which rarely sold out to its restricted audience of university teachers and other members of the professional class: half of the copies went directly to Latin America.

The *Biblioteca de ideas del siglo veinte* and the *Revista de Occidente* represent Ortega's tireless effort to bring European culture within range of the Spanish reader, in accordance with his belief that Spain's renaissance was contingent upon a marriage with Europe. He also made strenuous efforts to bring European personalities to Spain. Among others who spoke at the ILE's Residencia de Estudiantes in Madrid at Ortega's invitation were Bruce, who attempted to climb Mount Everest with Irving and Mallory; Howard Carter, who opened the tomb of Tutankhamun; and Albert Einstein, for whom Ortega acted as simultaneous translator.

The trajectories of the dictatorship and Ortega's life crossed in March 1929 when Primo closed down the universities as a response to student unrest. Ortega's reaction was to resign his chair at the University and to continue his philosophy course at the Cine Rex in the Calle Mayor. His opposition to the dictatorship was now clear, and his confidence in it as a salutary experience had evaporated. At this stage he could only fulminate against its having 'humiliated, trodden on, degraded and impoverished' the Spanish people during the seven years of its existence (OC 11, 177).

The Republic

In February 1931 Ortega threw himself behind the burgeoning Republican cause with the founding of the Agrupación al servicio de la república (Association at the Service of the Republic), his distrust of politics overshadowed by 'a rational decision that the exceptional historical circumstances in which he and his country found themselves gave the intellectual, the thinker, the theoretician and the teacher, an inescapable new social obligation' (in Durán, 1985:93).

The aim of the association, as expressed by Ortega and his co-founders Gregorio Marañón and Ramón Pérez de Ayala was,

to mobilise all Spanish intellectuals so as to form a large band of propa-
gandists for, and defenders of, the Spanish Republic. We call on all teachers,
writers and artists, doctors, engineers, architects and technical people of
all types, lawyers, solicitors and other men of law. Above all, we need the
collaboration of young people,   (OC 11, 127).

The intention was not to act as a political party but to liaise with all
other Republican groups in making the Republic an 'authentically
national' effort, in line with Ortega's idea that the country should
be run by a 'junta magna' of 200 of the best people drawn from all
walks of life. The aim of the Republic should be to 'waken our
people to a more energetic existence' (OC 11, 128) and to encourage
the provinces because 'We consider that the future of Spain depends
today on the provinces' (OC 11, 133). Practical – if not very
adventurous – weight was given to this assertion by Ortega, Marañón
and Pérez de Ayala when they gave their first public meeting in
Segovia rather than in Madrid – 'To begin in Segovia is a symbol
for us', said Ortega (OC 11, 133). He and his supporters thus
constituted one of the many groups and classes of people who had
their own idea of how the Republic would look and what it ought
to deliver.

In October 1929 Ortega had published the first article of what was
to be his most widely-read (and often misunderstood) book, *La rebelión
de las masas* (*The Revolt of the Masses*). Ortega intended 'masses' to be
a qualitative as well as a quantitative term but it is the latter denomination which has received most attention. There is no doubt that in these
terms Spain was changing fast by 1930. Between 1900 and 1930, with
the exception of Italy, Spain experienced the fastest population growth
in Europe (Martínez Cuadrado, 1983:80), and migration took increasing numbers of Spaniards to Madrid (p. 109), whose population nearly
doubled between those years (p. 121). Ortega's masses – especially
in the context of where he lived and worked – were not a figment
of his imagination.

But if the number of people in Spain had increased during this
period, the way in which the wealth was shared betwen them had not.
It was estimated in 1932 that about half of the land in Spain was owned
by just 10,000 families, and by 1933 in the province of Badajoz, 32.5
per cent of cultivated land was in the hands of 412 individuals
(Martínez Cuadrado, 1983:154). From the point of view of the
majority of those earning a living from the land, Spain had hardly
changed since Ortega first called for the country's modernisation. John

Langdon-Davies described the existence of the landless peasants of Extremadura in May 1936 in the following way:

At last we came to a low, long building which housed six families of human beings. These were the typical peasants of Extremadura. What we were to see could be seen a thousand times over almost without variation. At one end lived some *braceros*, men who did not own an animal and depended on being able to hire their own bodies out at harvest-time or seed-time to farmers needing manual labour. When in work they received one shilling a day. They had never tasted meat in their whole lives. They greeted us with the courtesy of any Spaniard. They talked and laughed with precisely the same brand of wit as Sancho Panza had. We went into a bedroom ten feet by ten, with a hole in the wall one foot square for a window. In this room, on sacking, slept night by night three married couples.

This was no dumping ground for down and outs; these were no worthless tramps, but typical representatives of the peasantry of Spain showing us their home. They had nothing to hope for; nothing else to remember when life ended. The universe of their personal experience would be square miles of parched untilled soil, and lost in the midst of the plain a room ten by ten shared between six grown men and women. (Langdon-Davies, 1937:39)

About 45 per cent of the population were still illiterate at this time, compared with 21.6 per cent in Italy, 41.9 per cent in Greece and some 3.5 per cent in the USA (Martínez Cuadrado, 1983:125). In short, Spanish society remained riven with inequality, injustice and tension as the Second Republic came into being on 14 April 1931.

Ortega considered agrarian reform and the Catalan statute to be 'the two great issues' confronting the Republic (OC 11, 456). The various measures which were introduced with regard to the first – tenants who could not pay rent were not ejected; in an attempt to diminish migration, employers were obliged to employ everyone available within a certain radius of the farm before looking elsewhere (this had the additional effect of preventing the undercutting of wages); an eight-hour day became standard; and protection against accidents at work was introduced – all depended for their eventual success or failure on the social relations which underlay them. These remained largely intact.

Ortega responded positively to Azaña's rationalisation of the way the Army was organised and the reduction in its top-heavy officer quotient, and it turned out to be a religious issue which first brought him into serious disagreement with the course the Republic was taking. Between 11 and 14 May various convents, churches and monasteries in Madrid and Andalucía were burnt down. Ortega wrote in *El Sol* that, 'burning convents and churches alone shows neither true Republican zeal nor a progressive spirit, but rather a primitive or criminal fetishism which is as likely to lead to the adoration of material things as to their destruction'. If the arsonists had been inspired by a new notion of democracy, he continued, 'they would not have burned the buildings, but rather proposed that they be used for social ends. If they were really modern men, the image of a Spain in flames – the Spain of the inquisitorial bonfire – would have prevented them from falling back into these stupid crematorial habits' (OC 11, 297–8).

On 5 August Ortega demanded that the Republic 'change direction' (OC 11, 363) and on 6 December he gave a radio broadcast entitled 'Rectificación de la república', or 'Correction of the Republic', while a book of the same name appeared on the 18th. On 9 September *Crisol* (financed by Urgoiti) published Ortega's famous verdict on the Republic: 'This is not it, this is not it!' (OC 11, 387).

In the spring of 1932, Ortega visited Tours and The Hague with his son Miguel but returned to Spain in time to speak in the Cortes during May and June on the Catalan question, supporting autonomy for Catalonia but not the full sovereignty that federalism would have implied: the latter would have caused too great a breach in his belief in a united nation. The theoretical underpinning for this view is discussed in chapter 5. The debate on the Catalan statute was to be his last major political contribution. In July he informed his son Miguel that, 'There is nothing we can do.' (Miguel Ortega, 1983:110), and in August, soon after the failed coup of General Sanjurjo, he resigned as deputy for León and Jaén and two months later the Agrupación was dissolved.

The Civil War

In June 1936 Ortega's son Miguel, wearing the traditional badges of *señoritismo*,[4] a jacket and tie, was shot at in a Madrid street. The military uprising which was to lead to the Civil War took place a month later, on 8 July. By 30 August Ortega, who was very ill with gallstones, was on his way out of Madrid with his family (helped by his brother Eduardo who was a socialist member of the Madrid City Council) bound for Alicante with two suitcases and 500 pesetas. In September

---

[4] Refers to the frivolous attitude and behaviour of young men from well-to-do families. A phenomenon particularly associated with early twentieth-century Spain.

he reached Marseilles and was in Paris by November. Nine years of full-time exile from Spain had begun, and from now until his death in 1955 he was never again in Spain long enough to be able to call it his home.

His public silence on the Civil War, the events leading up to it and what succeeded it, meant that one must refer to his private correspondence to gain some idea of his post-1936 political perspective, and I shall spend some time on this given the relative novelty of the information. The basic picture which emerges is that first, he wanted a Nationalist victory in the Civil War, and second, that his guardedly optimistic early view of the Franco regime gave way to disillusionment, particularly over the issue of censorship. Victor Ouimette has written that he kept his attitude toward the warring factions in Spain to himself 'although it is often assumed, on the basis of scanty evidence, that his sympathies lay with the Nationalists' (Ouimette, 1982:32). In my opinion, Ortega's correspondence of 1936–9 shows that this general assumption was correct, and that the evidence, based on material not used by or available to Ouimette, is substantial rather than scanty, as I hope to show.

On 1 September 1936, two days after Ortega had escaped to Alicante, *ABC* published a letter of support for the Republic signed by Ortega, Marañón, Pérez de Ayala, Machado, Menéndez Pidal and others. Here is Ortega's own account of the circumstances surrounding that event, as expressed in a letter to Victoria Ocampo. She has evidently invited him to stay in Argentina and he says that he cannot yet decide what to do:

The reason for my vagueness and obscurity is that the state of mind of the victorious forces once they take Madrid and begin, with that, to reconstruct Spain, cannot yet be made out. The thing is that my situation ought to be very favourable and that all those forces showed me deference and respect right up until the outbreak of war. The only thing they can hold against me is having had to sign a three-line manifesto declaring support for the Government of the Republic. But all of them know – and repeat – that that was something forced upon me under the most terrible threats. I absolutely refused to sign – I was very ill just then – another [manifesto] which attacked the military. But this refusal provoked the young Communist writers even more and they came back with new threats. Then I said that I would only sign three lines which did not offend anybody and which I could have signed a year before. And that is how it came out – I don't know who drafted it – completely different from the adjoining manifesto of the 'anti-fascist' writers, which underlined its [i.e. the piece he had signed] forced and unenthusiastic character.

For this reason the newspaper *Claridad* attacked me, blaming me – correctly – for this counterproductive outcome and revealing that 'my philosophy was that on which fascist minds had fed themselves'. I had to bear in mind that in those days such an accusation from that criminal newspaper was generally followed in twenty-four or forty-eight hours by a firing squad. However, I understood that beforehand they would want to force me to do something new so that my name could be used for their benefit. And so it was that they came back a few days later – with me in bed half-dying – to get me to talk to America on the radio! I got some of the more sensible ones to intervene and achieved a delay of which I managed to take advantage by escaping with my family, although I couldn't stand up. A couple of weeks later I, as a counter-revolutionary, was relieved of my chair by the 'purifying University Commission'.(FOG C. 186 JK 89/99 24.10.36)

Several things become clear on reading this very important letter. First, he thought a Nationalist victory likely even at this early stage and intimates that he would welcome it; second, he was by now fervently anti-Republican; third, he escaped from Madrid in fear of his life; and fourth, he was unsure as to how friendly his reception by the Nationalists would be. It is clear, too, that for those with political leanings there was no room in Spain at this point for half measures: one was either for or against the Nationalists.

Miguel Ortega tells us that in Paris his father followed the progress of the Civil War by drawing red and blue lines on a map of Spain, and in July 1937 Ortega wrote to the Condesa de Yebes from Holland that, 'I see that White Spain [i.e. Nationalist Spain] is becoming more orderly all the time, although at the expense of falling back under the influence of the usual forces' (FOG C. 199 JK 35/51 25.7.37). A month later, in one of his few direct references to Franco, he says, 'Although because of my stay in Holland I have very little information, my impression is also excellent – that is within the limits of what is possible and what is to be hoped for. Franco's statements are ever more sound and to the point' (FOG C. 203 JK 55/134 17.8.37).

On 26 April 1937 the most famous single event of the Civil War occurred: the bombing of Guernica by German Stuka dive-bombers. Pablo Picasso accordingly produced the War's most famous painting, which became both a symbol of the fight against fascism and a reminder of the brutality of war. In the same year he released an irreverent series of cartoons, for the most part depicting Franco sporting an oversize penis. It is unclear to which piece of work Ortega is referring in the following extract from a letter to the Condesa de

Yebes, but his contempt for the Republican cause is obvious: 'now I see that that idiot Picasso permits himself to produce doodles on the subject' (FOG C.199 JK 37/51 3.8.37). At the beginning of 1938 Ortega's son Miguel sent him the transcript of a speech given by Serrano Suñer, Franco's brother-in-law, and friend of José Antonio Primo de Rivera, founder of the Falange. In a letter, again to the Condesa, he writes of his enjoyment of the speech and notes, without complaint and with tacit satisfaction, that two-thirds of it seemed to have been taken directly from his own *España invertebrada* (FOG C.199 JK 40/51 10.4.38).

It is hard to read into his letters of this period anything other than a desire for a Nationalist victory. In May 1938, for example, he wrote of the fall of Tremp (which cut off Barcelona's supplies of hydroelectric power) that '[it] looks like being a re-run of Teruel [December 1937: when the Republican forces were made to beat a demoralising retreat] . . . I mean that another bout of depression like that which followed Teruel will put an end to resistance' (FOB C.199 JK 41/51 28.5.38). A final illustration of Ortega's partiality is drawn from a letter of February 1939, just nine days after the very last meeting of the Republican Cortes, and one day after Franco completed his occupation of Catalonia. In this letter Ortega consoles a friend whose son had died in the War with the thought that 'he did not die in an unlucky and meaningless accident, or of some stupid disease, but in a noble battle' (FOG C.203 JK 83/134 11.2.39).

La posguerra

The war of which this 'noble battle' was a part officially ended on 1 April 1939 and Ortega seemed relatively optimistic about future prospects: 'I don't have any hard information about Spain, but if we measure things as we ought – that is to say, knowing what is possible – my impression is not bad' (FOG C.199 JK 42/51 10.8.39). Nor, it appears, was he to change his mind for some time – until, in fact, he came face to face with the regime on the first of his visits to Spain in 1945. We might, nevertheless, hazard a guess that the fact that he did not return to Spain immediately after the Nationalist victory was secure, indicates that he had reservations either about the regime itself or the reception it might have given him.

After 1945 his letters began to include criticisms of the government, particularly with reference to censorship. He was evidently asked by a number of people to begin writing political commentaries again, and was in touch at various times with Italian, German and American newspapers while toying with the idea of writing a series of articles entitled 'Twenty years after' (FOG C.204 JK 105/134 26/7/47). The articles never appeared.

On a number of occasions Ortega expressed his disappointment at Spain's international isolation. In a letter to the Condesa de Yebes, for example, he writes: 'I see that the French frontier has opened up for you, and I imagine that you will try to cross to the other side. When this thing is finally sorted out and merchandise, too, can cross over, then I hope that the suffocating corner in which Spain lives will be aired a little. This confinement is one of the causes of my general bad temper during the last few months' (FOG C.199 JK 43/51 27.8.46). In July 1947 he referred to the 'vulgar stupidity' of the United Nations' continuing refusal to admit Spain to the organisation (FOG C.204 JK 106/134 26.7.47).

Ortega's unhappiness with the Franco regime developed, and in April 1946 he wrote to José Germaín:

Therefore, as far as politics is concerned, there is *no pretext* for not getting to work and doing things, as long as – of course – it has nothing to do with the activities of Government or which implies personal confidence in the Government, because it is clear that the Government does not deserve it and, moreover, that it is moribund.   (FOG C.204 JK 95/134 2.4.46)

By the middle of 1947 he says significantly that he is 'incompatible with Franco' (FOG C.204 JK 106/134 26.7.47), and was quoted in *Time* magazine's obituary on him as having said around this time that, 'I am here [in Spain], but I do not exist here. I do not want to take part in anything' (31 October 1955; p. 26). Four-and-a-half years later he expressed the extreme disillusionment – almost tiredness – which was to remain with him until his death:

On my visit to Madrid in December and January [1951–2] I found the city even more dejected than in the autumn, and it was already very dejected in the autumn . . . Without me being able to find the cause, motive or pretext, the government has become rougher, not only with us but with everyone. Along with this, although perhaps independent of that governmental attitude, the ecclesiastical censorship has been enormously extended in a way that we have not seen for some time. I repeat, no external cause, motive or pretext in our country justifies that.   (FOG C.208 JK 56/114 23.2.52)

The character of Ortega's work post-1936 was almost exclusively philosophical as opposed to political. We shall defer comment on this aspect until the latter part of this book, and in the meantime, a chronological list of his work may be found at the beginning. We cannot leave this section, however, without making mention of two enterprises in which Ortega became involved between the extraordinarily busy years of 1948 and 1950, and which provide an insight into the man's social thought throughout the period presently being considered.

The first was the Instituto de Humanidades, or Institute of Humanities, set up with Julián Marías in Madrid at the end of 1948. Marías himself informs us that the Instituto was founded under the auspices of his already existing Aula Nueva, because it was believed that the Franco government would not have countenanced the independent existence of a publicly recognised Institute co-founded by Ortega, who was by this time not particularly popular with the regime (Marías, 1983:399). The Instituto existed for two years, running courses on all aspects of the human sciences: philosophy, history, geography, literature, art and politics. Marías has commented that, 'The Instituto de Humanidades was the most important cultural phenomenon which had occurred since the beginning of the Civil War' (Marías, 1983:401), and although this may be a partisan comment, I believe it is true to say that, in terms of higher education, the enterprise represented the least ambiguous example of intellectual enquiry to be found in the Spain of that era.

Ortega's correspondence reveals that he hoped to take this enterprise abroad as well. In October 1951 after giving a lecture in Munich, he wrote the following to Jaime Benítez:

Although I only spoke about the project with very few people, the best of them turned out to be extremely enthusiastic. I won't say any more beyond the fact that such a shy and complicated character as Heidegger immediately came to see me in my hotel, full of enthusiasm and wanting to work with me. Much the same happened with Heisenberg. This means that it is no mere flight of fancy to think about gathering together here the most brilliant people in the world so as to work together on an 'Institute of Humanities'. That's to say that this city could aspire – for a few months – to being the genuine centre of intellectual life in the whole world.

(FOG C.207 JK 39/114 1.10.51).

The project itself foundered, principally for lack of money and because of Ortega's ill-health, but it is enough to mention the mere conception, in this context, in order to illustrate Ortega's favouring of the internationalisation of a liberal, humanistic and 'disinterested' education.

The second adventure of this period began in January 1949 when
Ortega received a letter inviting him to take part (for $5,000 and
travelling expenses) in the celebration, mentioned in the introduction, in Aspen, Colorado, of the bicentenary of Goethe's birth. The
organisers wrote to Ortega that: 'We are confident that our program
conforms with the aims that you have expressed with great eloquence
in your own works. We are convinced that you can consider the cause
of this Bicentennial Congress as your own cause.' And the cause?
'To help men to understand Goethe's wisdom and regain the world
perspective of a universal man. We hope that our program will contribute to the development of a world community' (FOG C.51 JK
69/75 21.2.49).

Ortega accepted the invitation to speak in Aspen, and appended
the following note to his letter: 'I read in a newspaper here that it
[his address] will have to be delivered in the evening, a fact I don't
dislike in the least, as our aim and end is precisely to fight darkness'
(FOG C.51 JK 74/75 7.6.49). The themes of the conference and
Ortega's ready acceptance to take part in it are, I believe, illustrative
of the general tenor of his social and political thought. This is not
the Ortega of the Civil War years in Paris, poring over his maps of
Spain, recording the satisfying advances of the Nationalist forces. Nor
is this the Ortega of 1923, welcoming the 'short, sharp shock' of Primo
de Rivera's dictatorship. This is the humanism and idealism of Ortega
being given free rein, allowing us, with hindsight, to count him among
those who saw themselves as constituting a bridgehead of civilisation
in the aftermath of the carnage of the Second World War. Both the
Instituto de Humanidades in Madrid, and the lectures he gave on
Goethe in America and Germany in 1949, constitute Ortega's contribution to that bridgehead. There are people alive today who will
testify to this, and to the tremendous effect that he had on his
audiences. Ortega was by all accounts a brilliant lecturer, and the
enormous numbers of people who listened to him throughout his life
– but particularly in post-war Europe – bear witness both to the
striking form and the relevant content of his words.

It is hard not to see something of the world citizen in Ortega
during these years away from home, visiting a large number of
countries and lecturing on humanistic subjects. In May 1953, for
example, he visited London after being invited to talk there by the
'Fund for the Advancement of Learning'. Among his colleagues at
the colloquium were the outstanding physicists, Niels Bohr and Werner

Heisenberg, both of whom have themselves come to stand for the principles of an ill-defined, but historically significant, humanistic liberalism. On 13 May Ortega wrote to his son José that Robert Hutchins had said that, 'he wanted me to go to America in the autumn with Heisenberg to get more formally involved in a new Institution which they want to create' (FOG C.208 JK 90/114 13.5.53). The journey was never made, but the enthusiasm with which he took up these suggestions and the energy with which he pursued them, at least while he was physically able, speak volumes for his political orientation in the period between the end of the Second World War and his death.

The ill-health which dogged Ortega from 1936 until his death prevented him from following up many of the projects of this post-war period, and this is another factor – besides patchy access to books and the very fact of exile itself – which ought to be borne in mind when considering the unevenness of Ortega's production between 1936 and 1955. Throughout the second half of 1954 he suffered particularly badly from stomach pains, and it is clear that a journey he made to Britain in October of that year to talk to the British Institute of Management in Torquay, not only bored him, but was a great strain on his health.

He spent the early summer of 1955 journeying through Italy, Germany and Switzerland and was back in Madrid by July, forced to return by Switzerland's prohibitive prices. One day not long after, in the offices of the *Revista de Occidente*, Ortega was planning for the journal's future with his colleagues: ' "Next year we're going to. . . ." Ortega grimaced imperceptibly, and Caro Baroja heard him murmur, "Next year I'll be pushing up daisies" ' (Rosa Montero, *El País semanal*, no. 316, p. 32). But he had given himself too long. By September his son Miguel, now a doctor, had diagnosed that he was suffering from advanced stomach cancer and gave him a month to live. An operation was proposed. Ortega was convinced that it would be nothing compared to the one that had saved his life in Paris in 1938. The operation never took place. He died on 18 October 1955, moments after complaining that everything had gone dark.

II

2

Socialism and capitalism

Political theorists have become accustomed to using the opposition
between individualism and collectivism as one way of categorising
political perspectives. There are, naturally, points of convergence,
but we feel entitled to make approximations according to whether a
theory holds that the isolated individual exists or whether he or she
is irremediably – and first and foremost – a part of a collective.
In these terms it can be instructive to place a thinker somewhere along
this spectrum, while it is particularly useful in Ortega's case because
of the variety which emerges. This variety, on the theoretical level,
is reflected in the strength of the support he accorded to socialism
or liberalism at the practical level.

In a conference he gave in Bilbao in 1910 he said that 'all individualism is mythology' and affirmed that, 'The isolated individual
cannot aspire to being man. The individual human being, separate
from society – as Natorp says – does not exist, he is an abstraction' (OC 1, 504).

Two points are being made here. The first is that one is not entitled to conceive of the 'isolated individual', for this view ignores the
context in which individuals find themselves – born into a particular
family and living in a specific society. To abstract the individual from
these circumstances is to misconstrue the nature of the human condition – a condition in which the individual is irrevocably situated
in a society. In the *Meditaciones del Quijote* (1914) he says 'How little
a thing would be if it were only what it is in isolation!' (OC 1, 350),
and his assertion that we must place each individual in the context
of a society is a reflection – at the level of political understanding
– of the analysis of 'structures' in the *Meditaciones*.

The second point to be made is captured in Ortega's assertion that

'The isolated individual cannot aspire to being man.' In saying this, he is borrowing from a line of thought with a long tradition: the idea that individuals cannot be fulfilled while they remain isolated. Aristotle's 'man is a political animal' who must live in a *polis* in order to be truly 'man' is close to Ortega's position. A major – and crucial – difference in the latter's prescription is that it *is* a prescription. Nowhere does he suggest that it is our natural, finished state to be in society, nor that there is something in our genetic makeup which drives us to form communities. Society, he says, was born of the fact that there were common tasks which needed to be achieved – 'if it was not essential for man to have certain products which can only be produced communally, society would not exist, and the world would be populated by recluses' (OC 1, 507). Our unity, then, comes from our work.

The communitarian nature of Ortega's early political thought was clearly a result of the influence of the social-democratic ideas of his mentors in Germany, Cohen and Natorp: indeed the debt to the latter is explicitly acknowledged above. In his search for a progressive ideology before the First World War, this communitarian perspective was always likely to lead him closer to socialism than, for example, to liberalism, although John Stuart Mill's 'No person is an isolated being' (*On Liberty*, p. 136) clearly leaves open the liberal option.

In any case, Ortega's own feeling was that the most important aspects of socialism were the 'assumptions of co-operation, of society, of the regime of living together' (OC 1, 509). The absence of any reference to a class analysis of society is significant. As it has been handed down to us, socialism generally involves some notion of the emancipation of the working-class, but this element receives practically no attention from Ortega – his use of socialism is highly eclectic.

Typically in this early period he defines himself as a socialist plus or minus something else (OC 10, 200 for example), but he is consistent on the point that socialism provides the new ideological context within which political thought must operate: 'Today, socialism has taken control of us, it dominates our reasoning, it orientates our political instincts, it provides the background for all our ideological combinations' (OC 10, 141). Again the reference to 'ideological combinations' reinforces the sense of a potential for eclecticism. It ought to be noted, though, that there is hardly a harsh word to be found about socialism or the Socialist Party in all of Ortega's writings. On the occasion of the election of Pablo Iglesias to the Cortes in 1910, Ortega referred to him as a 'lay saint'. He asserted, 'Today, whoever is not a socialist finds himself morally obliged to explain why he is not, or why he is not at least in part' (OC 10, 141), and in 1931, five months after the founding of the Second Republic when Ortega was already unhappy with the turn things were taking, he announced in a speech in the Cortes, 'At this time the political party which has the most strength in Spain – in terms of respect and number – is the Socialist Party. Why? Because it is the only one which, sacrificing its partisan interests, is behaving, not as would suit its immediate interest, but accepting what the moment demands beyond that interest' (OC 10, 441). Ortega, then, was practically always able to find time for socialism or the Socialist Party even if his defence of them was at the cost of substantial redefinition of the ideology.

In 1910, at least, his adherence seemed total: 'Today it is a scientific truth acquired *in aeternum* that the only morally admissible state is the socialist state', but the way in which the sentence finishes gives pause for thought: 'although I do not have to affirm that true socialism is that of Karl Marx, nor much less that the workers' parties are the only completely ethical parties' (OC 1, 509). This rider points us in the direction of the fissures that were evident between Ortega and socialist thought practically from the beginning of his career. Antonio Elorza provides the rubric: 'The Socialist Party, in Ortega's opinion, was failing to fulfill the Lassallian function of being an agent of national construction, above and beyond class solidarity, carried out by social democracy in Germany' (1984: 59).

Some of Marx's thought, and some of the tenets of socialism in general, were an irrelevance – even a hindrance – to Ortega's project of a renovated Spain. To be more specific we might turn to the issue of class, and to be more specific still, to the issue of class-struggle. The 'community' of which we have seen Ortega talking can clearly be defined in different ways. For Marx, the creating of a sense of community involved the creation of class-consciousness. The notion of a community of all the interests in society was anathema to him because he argued that such interests were irreconcilable under capitalism. Ortega's community, on the other hand, has nothing to do with pitting one class against another, but rather with uniting all classes in the task of the construction of a modern Spain. In this context, it was the modernity of socialism which appealed to Ortega, rather than what the ideology actually had to say. In a 1909 speech which he was invited to give by the Partido Socialista Obrero Español (PSOE), he made the following comment on the subject: 'I don't know if this is going to surprise you: you have been taught that the central formula of socialism is the class-struggle. For that reason I am not affiliated to your party, although my heart is a brother to yours. Only an adjective separates us: you, you are Marxist socialists; I, I am not a Marxist' (OC 10, 120). It is said that Marx claimed he wasn't a Marxist either, but it certainly was not because he did not believe in the class-struggle. Ortega, even at this early date, is distancing himself from what he refers to as the 'central formula of socialism'.

The 'principle of work'

A further gloss on this can be provided by referring to a long-running theme in Ortega's political thought: the principle of work – a principle which amounts to an attempt to gather everyone together in the enterprise of building the nation by appealing to them in a language which echoes socialism but which muddies its meaning. In the *El Sitio* speech of 1910 he says, 'If society is co-operation, then members of society have to be, before all else, workers. He who does not work cannot participate in society. This is the affirmation through which democracy is pinned down in socialism' (OC 1, 509). Three months earlier he had made it clear that he was not limiting himself to a proletarian definition of 'worker', nor even defining him or her in terms of a relationship with the owners of the means of production. Talking of the society he wanted to see, he said that, 'another of socialism's affirmations is that that society, that community, is only possible if we all make ourselves workers' (OC 10, 125). Now, if we adopt a 'by hand and brain' perspective of what it is to be a worker, we might accept Ortega's move beyond the concept of the manual worker as he or she is presented in the *Communist Manifesto* (for example), but with the idea of all of us being workers he has moved out of the orbit of what we normally understand to be democratic socialism and into the realms of 'national socialism'. The classic distinction between the owners of the means of production and those who work for them has been undermined with Ortega's assertion that even the former can sensibly be talked of as 'workers'. To this extent, his statement that it is an affirmation of socialism that socialist society 'is only possible if we all make ourselves workers' is disingenuous.

His 'principle of work' does, however, commit him to opposition to Spain's traditional aristocratic classes. He says that he wants to see a society organised legally 'according to the principle of work; that is, that there should exist no more individual wealth than that obtained by a person's own work' (OC 10, 583), and follows with the comment that the only people who could oppose such a principle would be 'small privileged minorities' (*ibid.*). Ortega, as a member of the rising bourgeois class, believed that the rule of the aristocrat should come to an end, but at the same time found himself being squeezed by an increasingly organised and influential working class. This Janus-faced position causes him to take on the trappings of socialism as the most promising modernising ideology available; using it to attack the traditional locus of political power (the aristocracy), while massaging its language to steer it away from exclusively working-class territory. Ortega's difficulty is that he is searching for a set of political ideas which will perform the liberating function of liberalism in late seventeenth- and eighteenth-century England, but is confronted by a completely different historical situation: the extent of the role of the state had become a feature of political discourse, and the working class, although small, had a more sophisticated organisation – was more conscious of itself as a class – than its eighteenth-century English counterpart. Neither traditional liberalism nor traditional socialism, then, will do.

Nationalism, internationalism and the 'trickle-down' theory

The national focus of Ortega's political thought provides the ground for another point of departure from socialism. It was one of Marx's maxims that a characteristic of the proletariat as a class is that it is international. I think it is fair to say that this maxim has been handed down, albeit in watered-down form, even to today's parliamentary, 'democratic' form of socialism: prolonged strikes by groups of workers in one country receive support from workers in other countries. But in Ortega's day the internationalist character of the proletariat had a much higher profile: the arguments about whether socialism in one country was possible were indeed already raging, but orthodox socialism had adopted internationalism as its byword, and the position was that the proletarian had no country, but only class.

Ortega's position on this issue is unequivocal and it provides us with another measure of his distance from the ideology of socialism, while ostensibly associating himself with it. He says that 'the aspirations of the proletariat' can only be achieved 'through national construction' (OC 10, 204), and goes on to paraphrase Marx himself in his own support: 'The full development of the capitalist structure is the [only] condition under which socialism can seriously entertain the hope of triumph' (*ibid.*). Placing this statement in a national context allows Ortega to argue for the development of capitalism in Spain as a necessary condition for the advent of (what he calls) socialism.

Marx's statement, however, is open to at least two interpretations. His position is that the development of capitalism is indeed the condition for socialism, but that this is because capitalism contains the seeds of its own destruction: the contradictions within the capitalist productive process must be fully expressed before the proletarian revolution ushers in the era of socialism. Marx, in other words, envisages not only the development of capitalism, but also its destruction, as the precondition for socialism.

Ortega, however, stops short of the second precondition. His position – defended from beginning to end – is that the development of capitalism will increase the sum of material wealth at society's disposal – wealth from which the working class will ultimately benefit. His is none other than an expression of what has come to be known as the 'trickle-down' theory: that the richer a society is the better it is for all concerned, regardless of class relations, because the wealth will eventually 'trickle down' through all levels. From this perspective flow certain consequences, not all of which square with traditional socialist thought.

For example, it is possible to demonstrate that strikes, far from being the only effective weapon which the working class has at its disposal with a view to improving conditions, are in fact counterproductive. They are counterproductive first, because they disrupt the productive process and second, because this disruption reduces the country's money-making potential which is to everybody's disadvantage – even, ultimately, the working class itself.

In reply, then, to socialism's internationalism, Ortega maintains that a socialist party should take into account the specific conditions of the country in which it operates before deciding upon a course of action:

In the countries at the forefront of capitalist evolution, the party is left with hardly anything to do except obtaining the best conditions for the worker. Those countries cannot be richer than they are, nor can they be better served than they are in all technical matters. What can the worker do? Only intervene as a worker. As a proletarian. Everything else is given to him without his intervention. Put another way: the German worker suffers as a worker, but not as a German. (OC 10, 204)

But, he says, clearly with Spain in mind, what happens 'if a modern nation is not yet a completely modern nation?' (*ibid.*). The answer is as follows: 'The less developed their respective nations are, the more national socialist parties have to be' (OC 10, 206). This is another indication of Ortega's intention to push socialism into the service of national construction rather than working-class emancipation. Incidentally, he was convinced that the First World War would signal the end of the idea of internationalism and initiate a healthy revival in national feeling: 'This year,' he wrote on 1 May 1915, 'the international workers' festival has been broken . . . rich and poor will live this day together in the trenches of France, Belgium, Poland and Galicia. A good lesson for all those workers to learn – that things are not as simple as Karl Marx thought' (OC 10, 309).

It is worth noting that here, in amongst the specifically political comment, we have come across an example of Ortega's general reluctance to indulge in utopias, and to take account of 'what is' in deciding what ought to be on the political agenda. If the actual conditions do not contain the seeds of success of a particular programme, then the programme will inevitably founder. Ortega thought that socialism's 'abstract' internationalism, born of its notions of an international proletariat, constituted just such a programme – particularly in the Spanish context: 'The day when Spanish workers abandon abstractions and recognise that they suffer, not only as proletarians, but also as Spaniards, they will make the Socialist Party the strongest party in Spain' (OC 10, 206). The same sentiment is echoed in the following comment on the *Communist Manifesto*: 'The *Communist Manifesto* is a brilliant work of illusionism and attraction, but no more. Reality has taken its revenge, as it will do with every attempt to replace what is lived and concrete with what is thought and abstract' (OC 10, 651). The significance of this statement in the context of Ortega's thought goes way beyond politics and takes us into the final part of this book. Here, though, it provides us with further space between Ortega and socialism in general, and between him and Marx in particular – differences that can nearly always be traced back to his desire to marshal socialism as an ideology of national construction.

Capitalism

It is clear from what we have said that capitalism, itself, has a key role to play in such construction, but at other levels Ortega has an ambivalent attitude towards it. His resilient humanism leads him to baulk at the undignified materialism and acquisitiveness which capitalism brings in its train, burying the spiritual aspects of human existence: 'Nineteenth-century capitalism has demoralised humanity. Doubtless it created fabulous material wealth, but it has impoverished the ethical consciousness of man' (OC 10, 673). At the same time Ortega reserves some of his harshest words for the new class thrown up by capitalism: 'It is the *petit-bourgeois* who stops history being made because his ambition is reduced to hoping that each day is as identical as possible to all the others. His only sensuality is the daily grind' (OC 11, 94). Capitalism, Ortega is saying, stunts ambition and provides for a mean, petty and materialistic morality; all of which is summed up in the character and activity of the *petit-bourgeois*, the entrepreneur *par excellence*. Nor do other classes escape this domination of the human by the material: 'This is Marx's clear and deep vision: that the human, which is pure quality, lies oppressed by quantity, which is a physical force' (OC 10, 239) and, 'The worker, as an individual, as quality, as heart, disappears; only a quantity remains. The worker not only lives on a daily wage, he *is* a daily wage' (OC 10, 240).

All of this indicates that Ortega's opinion of capitalism is highly ambiguous. On the one hand he rejects its materialism and the way in which it demands what he sees as small-mindedness in the people who live in its shadow. On the other hand he knows that the modernisation, construction and 'Europeanisation' of Spain demands that advantage be taken of capitalism's fabulous productive potential.

This indeterminacy is neatly expressed in his attitude to the material demands made by the dispossessed working class. He agrees, from one perspective, with the socialist belief that 'today's society is committed to arbitrariness and is unjustly organised in an economic sense' (OC 10, 588), and is prepared to go along with working-class demands for a fairer distribution of the material wealth which capitalism provides. But at the same time we have seen him bemoaning the acquisitive human being nurtured by such demands.

Equality and hierarchy

While he would have welcomed an improvement in the material conditions of the working class, Ortega baulked at the notion of a classless, even egalitarian society. Hierarchy is a theme that runs right through his work and he has both a descriptive and a prescriptive attitude towards the concept. His opinion is that hierarchies constitute an inalienable structure of human existence – such existence is characteristically hierarchic, and that is that. Further, given his maxim that what is has to be taken into account in deciding what ought to be done, his prescriptive position is not so much one of whether to do away with hierarchies or not (for that is impossible), but rather to accept that society will be hierarchical and to organise it in such a way that its hierarchy most adequately reflects its underlying structure.

In terms of the terrain which we are presently covering, Ortega has the following to say: 'I am a socialist for love of the aristocracy' (OC 10, 239), and continues, 'Aristocracy means a social system in which the best (*los mejores*) have a decisive influence' (*ibid.*). For Ortega, the problem with capitalism is that it produces an aristocracy based on 'a material, anonymous, quantitative power: money' (*ibid.*). He sees hope in socialism because its 'historical mission' is to 'overcome, conquer, and annihilate capitalism', and from this it is clear that for Ortega socialism's job is not to supersede capitalism because it produces inequalities, alienation, and irrational production and distribution, but because it produces the wrong sort of aristocracy. The mission of socialism is not to remove hierarchies from the agenda but to make possible a different sort. Ortega's aristocracy of culture cuts across social divisions and while he might like to see the latter disappear (although this is never explicit), he does not want to see the hierarchy implied by the former disturbed. With the passing of capitalism, he says, 'Classes will return, who doubts that? But they will not be economic classes; men will not be divided into rich and poor, but into best and worst. Art, Science, Refinement and Moral Energy will once again be social values' (OC 10, 240).

Socialism, culture and the state

Much of what we have seen so far of Ortega's opinions on socialism and capitalism are a reflection of his belief that Spain's problem was a problem of culture. In this particular context he says, 'For me, socialism is culture' (OC 10, 120). Once again, he is steering socialism away from what we might normally understand by it towards a meaning which suits the use he wants to make of it.

From this perspective, the improvement of material well-being is a means to an end, not an end in itself, although he does indicate, by quoting from a French poet, that a minimum material standard of living is required for culture to be possible:

> When you have enough to pay the rent
> You can start thinking about being virtuous.

And continues, 'For that reason, the first thing that we have to try to do is to make the social economy more just' (OC 10, 124).

At this point Ortega, momentarily at least, comes close to working from the perspective of a positive, socialistic conception of freedom. Traditional liberal notions would have it that freedom has an essentially negative character – freedom *from* interference in one's own private space, either by other individuals or by the state. This is the point of view represented by John Stuart Mill (among others) when he says in *On Liberty* that 'the sole end for which mankind are warranted, individually or collectively, in interfering with the liberty of action of any of their number, is self-protection. That the only purpose for which power can be rightfully exercised over any member of a civilised community, against his will, is to prevent harm to others' (p. 72). We shall see Ortega presenting a very similar idea on various occasions, but in his comment referred to above he is implicitly acceding to greater interference than Mill would allow, in the name of the 'necessity' of giving 'all men the possibility of being fully men'. The substantive point is that on this reading it is not enough simply to attach certain abstract rights to human beings by virtue of their being born (life, liberty and the pursuit of happiness, for example), but also to create the conditions in which those rights can be concretely fulfilled.

From this perspective, the role of the state in political affairs inevitably arises as a subject for discussion, and provides us with another landmark in Ortega's political geography. The question of the extent of state intervention arises from socialism's observation that traditional liberal *laissez-faire* economics results in unacceptable margins of inequality – margins which mock liberalism's claim to be a philosophy of freedom for everyone. Socialism's position is that the state should be used to reduce those margins of inequality, to which the liberal replies that such intervention by the state engenders the individual's 'private-space liberty' by obliging him or her, for instance, to pay income tax so as to finance a state welfare system.

To this extent, Ortega perfectly sums up the opposition between liberalism and socialism with the following remark: 'Socialism, by proclaiming the interventionist principle (of the state) presents itself with Lassalle as the born enemy of individualist liberalism' (OC 10, 201). He continues by explaining that liberalism advocates the absence of the state from civil society so as to preserve the state's impartiality. This would be fine, he says, in an abstract situation, but the fact is that the state *has* interfered in civil society and has produced inequalities. If it were now to stay out of civil society, 'it would achieve no more than the growth of the inequalities which it has itself produced' (*ibid.*). His conclusion is that 'The only fair posture for the state would be to intervene against its past interventions and destroy privilege, because privilege means favours given by the state' (*ibid.*). Leaving aside the question of whether Ortega is right to say that it is the state which has created privileges, or whether they are rather the result of a whole socio-economic system of which the state is but a part, his position on the role of the state, as expressed here, appears to be unashamedly socialist.

However, the signs are there that this is not a wholehearted commitment to the principle of state intervention. Rather than an ideological belief, Ortega's posture is based on his maxim, upon which we have commented, that what is must be taken into account in deciding what ought to be. He is saying that state intervention is a fact of political life and we should begin from there. True, he says (here in 1913) that it should be used to reduce margins of inequality, but that is a comment on inequality, not on the limits of the role of the state *per se*.

This rather negative justification of state intervention – i.e. that the state should intervene because it already does – is consistent with Ortega's general position on the question. Around the time of 'Old and new politics' (1914) ideas of traditional liberal 'private-space liberty' become more prominent in his work and freedom *from* interference takes over from freedom *to* develop as a fully human being. A comment he made in 1919 is representative of the shift: 'socialism, as well as being socialist, is democratic and liberal. The State of which it conceives does not permit dictatorship and guarantees the liberty of the citizen' (OC 10, 588). The juxtaposition of 'dictatorship' with 'liberty' indicates the kind of liberty to which he is referring: freedom from interference. From this point on we hear more of the freedom of the individual from restraint and less of the freedom which every individual should have to fulfil his or her potential – a theme which will recur in the next chapter.

We can put a final gloss on this issue by saying that although we have seen Ortega insisting that material well-being is an essential precondition for culture, his most general position involves reversing the terms – a position reflected in his practical political enterprises. His assessment of Spain's problem as cultural led him to propose cultural solutions. This emphasis on a revival of culture and education derives from the idea of the need to fill a spiritual reservoir, and stands against the materialist conception of history which holds that culture is dependent on the relations between the owners and the workers of the means of production, and that culture can only be changed or augmented *via* an alteration of those relations.

The concrete form that Ortega's belief in culture and education as data independent of socio-economic relations took was, of course, the Liga de educación política, founded in 1913. In 1908 he had said, 'An Indian poem speaks of a hermit whom the Gods threw out of the heaven of Indra. Through the power of his thought and the strength of his spiritual concentration, the hermit created a new world and a new heaven. Similarly, I believe that no other option but this remains open to the Spanish people' (OC 10, 77). The Liga was the concrete expression of this option, and it is probably fair to say that its failure was partly a result of the shortcomings of such an option. 'Spiritual concentration', on its own, was not enough to effect the kind of change Ortega was looking for. The Liga as a political project was characterised by a naivety which one would not expect of someone operating according to the following maxim: 'The only thing which ought to be is that which can be, and the only thing which can be is that which is already developing within what is.' The organisation, in sum, was a utopian initiative of the type which Ortega so often criticised.

Conclusion

In 1915 Ortega wrote that 'Every individual who knows how to be faithful to himself manages to compose a highly personal religion. And on the first of May it is a ritual act of my religion to park myself on the corner of La Equitativa and watch the workers go by' (OC 10, 307). In terms of socialism as an ideology of egalitarianism and working-class emancipation he was never more than an observer. Despite his (albeit short-lived) reverence for Pablo Iglesias and his exhortation to those who were not socialists to explain why not, his enthusiasm for socialism was exhausted by its potential as an ideology of organisation and modernisation in which the solidarity of class is replaced by the community of the nation, and the equality of all human beings is discarded in favour of a form of social–cultural aristocracy. A recognition of this should help to put comments such as the following into perspective: 'Upon his return from Germany [1908], and simultaneous with his entrance into public life, Ortega's sympathies for socialism became manifest' (Ouimette, 1982: 22). Marx, in the *Communist Manifesto*, provides a succinct epitaph for the tombstone of Ortega's socialism: 'the Socialistic bourgeois want all the advantages of modern social conditions without the struggles and dangers that would necessarily result. They desire the existing state of society minus its revolutionary and disintegrating elements. They wish for a bourgeoisie without a proletariat.' It would be interesting, further, to place Ortega's 'socialism' in the context of that of the PSOE itself during this period, with particular reference to its poverty of theory (see Heywood: 1986) and its poor relations with sympathetic intellectuals. Such a task properly done, however, would take us beyond the rubric of this chapter and this present book.

Much of Ortega's relationship to socialism is informed by his ambivalent attitude towards capitalism. His nervousness at what the capitalist ethic was doing to human sensibility never overcame his desire to see a modern Spain and his opinion that a modern Spain would to some extent be a capitalist Spain: 'It seems to us . . . foolish to frighten the capitalists' (OC 11, 142), he said two months before the Second Republic came into being.

3

Liberalism and democracy

The rejection of the 'isolated individual' noted at the beginning of the last chapter clearly puts Ortega at odds with practically all interpretations of the liberal tradition. At the heart of liberalism lies the idea of the individual's private space which no one or no thing is permitted to invade except under very specific circumstances. The circumstances vary according to the liberal tradition with which one is dealing, but the private space is common to all. Ortega's 'man is completely social' (OC 1, 511) denies any conception of private space – indeed it implies that any suggestion to the contrary is based on a misunderstanding of the human condition.

This phase of his thought, however, is in truth very circumscribed. In fact the structural sense he gives to the social nature of human beings by referring to it as a part of the human condition is beginning to be undermined as early as 1914 when 'perspectivism' makes its first implicit appearance in the *Meditaciones*. The individualistic implications of perspectivism (with which we shall be dealing in detail in the final part of this book) are so profound that it is sometimes hard to see anything public coming out of it at all. In 1916, in an article called *Verdad y perspectiva* ('Truth and perspective'), he explains that, 'each man has a mission of truth. Where my eye is, there is no other: what my eye sees of reality no other eye sees', and that, 'Reality gives itself up in individual perspectives' (OC 2, 19). This epistemological individualism clearly tears the seamless web of social life to which Ortega subscribed in 1910.

Even as early as 1910, in fact, Ortega allows expressions of individualism to find their way into his discourse at the political level – expressions, moreover, of a very particular sort of individualism. In the Bilbao conference he says that he has very little time for 'rights of man' style individualism: 'Maybe there are some people who are happy with that empty form of individualism which comes

58

with being born and on which are based the rights of man. This legal self which exists in the mind, and which constructs the emptiness of equality, is all very well – but it is not enough.' This is a significant sentiment. Not only is Ortega preparing us for some sort of individualism, albeit not the one which we might expect, he is also distancing himself from the egalitarian form of individualism implicit in the notion of *everyone* having certain rights by virtue of being born. In this way he is avoiding relations with what I think it is fair to characterise as a dominant tradition of liberalism – which implies equality even if it takes second place to individual liberty – in favour of . . . what?

He makes his intentions clearer with the following remark: 'True individualism lies in this direction: not to be different but to become different.' It will not escape notice that the dynamism to which Ortega refers has as its aim a differentiation between human beings. These notions of 'difference' and the 'emptiness of equality' are close to the heart of a certain type of meritocratic individualist liberal political thought, and they point us, *grosso modo*, in one direction which Ortega's political thought was to take.

This tension between individualism and collectivism also led Ortega to dabble with something he called 'socialist liberalism': 'the only possible liberalism today is socialist liberalism' (OC 10, 377). This idea seems confused in that if liberalism is socialist then it is no longer liberal, but behind the confusion lie indications of the source of his concern with both unadulterated socialism and liberalism. The following quotation makes the point clear: 'It seems that either we have forgotten, or we have never known, that the true liberals – those of the nineteenth century – were men who formed majorities but legislated for minorities. That is liberalism – magnanimous politics' (OC 10, 169). Liberalism, then, without the community of socialism; and socialism, without the concern for minorities typical of liberalism, are both insufficient and inadequate.

With remarks of this sort Ortega is placing himself firmly in the kind of frame of reference supplied by John Stuart Mill when he introduced his *On Liberty* by explaining that it was concerned with 'the nature and limits of the power which can be legitimately exercised by society over the individual' (p. 65). Mill goes on to suggest that 'the individual versus society' is a special case of a more general issue – i.e. the minority versus the majority – and continues: 'in political speculations "the tyranny of the majority" is now generally included among the evils against which society requires to be on its guard' (p. 68). Ortega is clearly equally concerned with the danger majority rule presents to minorities, and this is the reason why his characterisation of liberalism as a 'magnanimous politics' makes it attractive to him.

Further, the generosity of liberalism reflected both his style and his conviction, for he is constantly shy of the destructive, uncreative spirit which lies at the heart of unalleviated criticism. At one point in *On Liberty*, John Stuart Mill says, 'If all mankind minus one were of one opinion, and only one person were of the contrary opinion, mankind would be no more justified in silencing that one person, than he, if he had the power, would be justified in silencing mankind' (p. 79). The sentiments of tolerance, open-mindedness and generosity which inform Mill's conclusion are central to what it was about liberalism that Ortega found attractive.

Democracy, liberty and the state

It has been pointed out by others that Mill's generosity in the face of the claims of individuals and minorities led him to be suspicious of democracy in terms of its implications of majority rule, and Ortega occasionally follows the same pattern. His basic position is that democracy and liberalism are answers to two different questions: democracy deals with the question of who should be sovereign (the people), and liberalism deals with the question of the limits of sovereign power. One might think that because they deal with different questions, the two principles would only rarely come into conflict, but Ortega's 1932 characterisation of democracy leads to a different conclusion: 'that sovereign Power of unlimited extension is characteristic of pure democracy – of that democracy which is nothing else but democracy, and which being only democracy is antiliberal. That unlimited sovereign Power has always been constitutive of pure democracy (which ours is not: ours is liberal) from the time of Pericles up until today's communism' (OC 11, 480).

The reason why liberalism and democracy come into conflict here is because Ortega has chosen to see democracy in terms of a system which implies unlimited power, which in turn becomes unlimited *state* power. This is not the only way in which to conceive of democracy (witness theories of participatory democracy which allow for local participation, thus undercutting the possibilities of excessive state involvement), but having decided to do so, Ortega has created a tension between liberalism and democracy, with the former acting as a check on the authoritarian tendencies of the latter. The relationship between liberalism and democracy has become the relationship between the individual and the state by the expedient of defining democracy in terms of unlimited state power. The movement in his political thought can now be traced through an analysis of the relative weights he gives to either the state or the individual.

To a large extent this relationship depends on whether he is dealing with a negative or a positive notion of liberty. In the last chapter it was noted that a negative conception involves freedom from interference, while a positive conception has to do with the freedom to fulfill one's potential as a human being. Further, it was seen that the latter conception generally involves state intervention in the affairs of individuals, for instance to raise taxes to provide a comprehensive system of education. Ortega vacillates between both conceptions of political freedom.

For instance, in 1908 we find him rejecting as inadequate what Unamuno called 'anarchistic liberalism' with its stress on the freedom of the individual from interference: 'Liberty is awareness of the law, and the law is social. Liberalism is everywhere in crisis and that is because what is also in crisis is the Manchesterian conception of the law which produced the classic school of political economy – the true essence of liberalism – which has, at bottom, been anarchistic up to now' (OC 10, 82). The *laissez-faire* economic doctrines propounded by the Manchester economists were based on a conception of political freedom encapsulated in the notion of freedom from interference, and the idea that individual improvement was the concern of the individual alone. This stress on self-help rendered the state practically redundant as a source of well-being for the community – indeed the only state involvement which could be justified was that which would ensure free and fair competition in the market. Ortega's 1908 rejection of the 'Manchesterian conception of the law' can be taken as a repudiation of these kinds of ideas.

A year later, he produced a description of two kinds of liberty, the second of which takes us into territory prohibited by the Manchesterian conception, and which Ortega was prepared to enter – at least for the time being: 'as far as we are concerned liberty ought to imply a double obligation on the individual, to act with absolute fairness, and on the state, to give the individual an ever better opportunity to make use of that liberty' (OC 10, 113). This second meaning is evidently at odds with the Manchesterian school – and thus with early liberalism – because of its recognition of the role of the state in the affairs of the individual. Far from being a threat to liberty, the state – on this reading – acts as a catalyst in bringing about its fulfilment, by creating the conditions in which the abstract liberty of the rights of 'man' can be made concrete for all 'men'. This role for the state evidently takes Ortega into territory normally occupied by the collectivist wing of liberal thinkers: 'the State should organise that progressive elevation of the working class' (OC 10, 470).

The role of the state in this picture is clear and unambiguous – and illiberal in the traditional sense of the word. It is, however, consonant with the views of liberals in Britain during the 1880s and 1890s whom Stuart Hall has referred to as the 'architects of the early welfare state' (Donald and Hall, 1986: 36) – liberals who muted the strident *laissez-faire* principles of their traditional counterparts. The notions of state intervention and the providing of conditions for the fulfilment of positive freedom which we have seen Ortega entertaining, place him squarely in this 'new liberal' tradition – a response to the pressures on society created by industrialisation and the political and economic demands of the working class.

This sort of liberalism entails a rejection of the radical individualism which forms the basis of classical liberalism. Ortega sees the latter liberalism as an essentially destructive force, shattering the bonds and fetters of medieval society and making way for mobility and enterprise. Writing in 1910 he expresses the opinion that classical liberalism has fulfilled its historical function, and that now is the time for a more constructive initiative to be taken – an initiative represented by democracy. Democracy should not deny the conquest of the concept of individual rights by liberalism, he says, but,

its mission is to go beyond it while preserving it. Individual rights were instruments which served to chip the citizen away from the rough block of the old State. Its value was purely negative; such rights are not principles of organisation or social construction. They were liberal because they freed people from the old regime, and their meaning will survive as a precaution against a possible return to it. Democracy contributes constructive and organic principles.   (OC 10, 170)

To this extent, democracy's job is to provide the sense of organisation and community absent from the competitive individualism characteristic of traditional liberalism. It ought to be noted that this is a very end-orientated version of democracy: Ortega's notion of the importance of 'rule by the people' is that is gives a sense of the 'people' where before there was only a sense of 'persons'. There have been (and are) traditions of democratic thought which hold that the means inherent in democratic politics are more important than the ends it achieves, in that participation in the democratic process makes for a more fulfilled people. There is no sense of this in Ortega: just as socialism was dragooned into the service of national construction, so democracy's sole purpose is to provide a sense of society above and beyond the demands of particular individuals or groups.

Ortega's criticism of the private, then, which we noted at the beginning of this chapter, leads him to value the public, the community, and to search for a principle which will embody these ideas. To this extent, democracy acts as a counterbalance to the individualism of liberalism. Consequently, liberal democracy, as we might expect, finds favour with Ortega and he says that 'such a way of life will not be the best imaginable, but any better life that we care to imagine will have to preserve the essence of those principles' (*Rebelión*: 97).

On occasion, however, Ortega's support for these principles – particularly the second – comes unstuck. We remember his characterisation of pure democracy as a 'sovereign Power of unlimited extension' (OC 11, 480), which he then tends to slide over into identifying with the worst features of unlimited state power. In this way, democracy becomes a potential threat to the freedom of the individual from state intervention. We have also seen that his support for state intervention depended upon a specific conception of political freedom: that abstract 'rights of man' freedom is empty so long as one is deprived of the material means to enjoy that freedom. From time to time, this defence of the role of the state is undermined by Ortega's subscription to a different notion of political freedom.

This different notion is captured in the following expression: 'The first half of the nineteenth century, guaranteeing the results of the French Revolution, conquered this "right to distance", which is nothing other than political liberty' (OC 10, 329). Political liberty, on this reading, is exhausted by the idea of every individual having the right to a private space, secure from violation either by the state or by other individuals. The extent of this space has been debated by liberal theorists down the years, but it is not a question with which Ortega deals. It is enough to see that he recognises the existence of this conception of political liberty, and that it is a conception firmly rooted in the liberal tradition – Mill makes it a central theme of his work: 'Over himself, over his own body and mind, the individual is sovereign' (*On Liberty*, p. 73).

Ortega's recognition, of course, does not necessarily amount to support for the private-space liberty of liberalism. But bearing in mind his version of pure democracy as absolute state power, it may be surmised that democracy, as a principle, might come into conflict with liberty, as defined above. Ortega reminds us that democracy asks a different question to liberalism ('who ought to rule', rather than 'what are the limits of power'), and then continues:

Perhaps it is the best [answer to the question of who ought to rule], but until that question is resolved in one way or another, I need, naturally, without distinction, ambiguity or reservation, to keep my personality intact. To know that whoever is ruling – a Prince or the people – nobody will be able to have control over what is inalienable in me. Liberalism and democracy, then, are not only two different things, but also one is much more important than the other.   (OC 10, 329–30)

This sentiment constitutes a considerable backing-down from his position on freedom and the role of the state identified earlier, and it has been achieved by reversing the sign of freedom (positive to negative, fulfilment to integrity) and positing democracy as a threat to this different, negative freedom. The point is that Ortega is demonstrating himself capable of retreating into a classical liberal conception of freedom, which commits him to privileging liberty (of a very specific type) over equality. This, of course, is one of the determinants by which we distinguish between socialism and liberalism. Ortega's position here is unequivocally liberal.

Nor is this a piece of isolated speculation on his part. At another point he says, 'Before being workers, or if you like, at the same time as being workers, we are human beings and, as such, we have a series of basic rights prior to any political organisation which the latter must guarantee us. The sum of these rights is called liberty' (OC 10, 594). As a statement of the liberal conception of rights and liberty this could hardly be bettered, and it also serves to place Ortega in clear opposition to the socialist critique of liberalism which holds that the 'abstract rights of human beings' constitute a concept which serves to consolidate bourgeois rule. While claiming rights for everybody, the bourgeoisie denies the proletariat the conditions in which they can be exercised. Ortega is now less concerned with the conditions than with the rights. He concludes that 'individual liberty . . . is for us the first and the last in politics' (OC 10, 596).

It is tempting to try to produce a chronological pattern of Ortega's move from a conception of positive political freedom and the state intervention that that implies, to a more negative notion of traditional liberal private-space liberty. But even a cursory glance at the dates of his remarks make such a project unworkable. To take two examples at random, his recommendation that the state should involve itself in raising the standard of living of the working class (OC 10, 470) was made in 1918, while the expression of his desire to 'keep his personality intact' and the consequent privileging of liberalism over democracy (OC 10, 329–30), dates from 1915.

This stands against the traditional interpretation of his thought which has it that his early 'socialist' phase corresponds to a support for state intervention, which gave way to a 'liberal' phase in which equality was sacrificed to a stress on individual liberty. I think that a more fruitful way of approaching the problem is to see that Ortega was in a genuine quandary. His desire to see a modernised, economically vibrant Spain, with all the organisation by the state that that may imply, occasionally came into conflict with his concern to preserve the freedom of the individual from state intervention. In neither wanting to give away the ground captured by individualist liberal theorists, nor believing that Spain's recovery could take place without state involvement, Ortega found himself on the horns of a dilemma. This is why the variety of his pronouncements on the relative importance of state intervention and individual freedom is best seen as a tension rather than as conceptions which succeed one another chronologically in his thought.

Problems with democracy

Ortega was never a robust defender of democracy and his first concern with it was that he believed the numerical method of arriving at decisions to be inadequate: 'The opinion of the majority is a numerical notion which says nothing of the energy or capacity for execution associated with the opinion' (OC 10, 190). Ortega does not explain how the 'energy' behind an opinion might be calculated, but it is a short step from this kind of statement to the abandonment of the principle of one person one vote. In *Representative Government*

John Stuart Mill argues in favour of a system of plural voting in which some people (the more intelligent ones) would be entitled to a greater weight of vote than others, and although Ortega never makes such a specific recommendation, it is clear that, on this score at least, he is as much of a reluctant democrat as was Mill.

A second worry which Ortega expresses with regard to democracy is its threat to competence. Writing in February 1918, he says that before the First World War, 'The conviction that Parliament meant the defeat of competence and the triumph of men of secondary quality was felt by nearly everybody' (OC 10, 392). The reason for this fear for competence, according to Ortega, is that all that is required of parliamentarians is that they get elected, and it does not necessarily require great talents of statesmanship to achieve this. In other words, the competence of politicians in a parliamentary democratic system is restricted to vote-winning, whereas what their job should demand of them is that they be competent to decide upon a policy for the nation. Ortega's concern for competence is deepened by one of the consequences of a democratic system – that governments come and go. This means that ministers, he says, require between six and ten months to accustom themselves to their departments before they can run them properly. Ortega, with no small dose of cynicism, says that, 'Some friends of mine call this democracy' (OC 10, 394). In both of these cases his emphasis on competence is in danger of overriding any democratic instincts he might entertain.

From time to time one feels that these criticisms of the parliamentary system are aimed more at the individuals it tends to throw up, than to the system itself. In this context, Ortega says: 'There is no choice but to restore the authority of Parliament. With some modifications here and there, Parliament is an inevitable institution, and the one most suitable for our times' (OC 11, 22). It is hard to see what modifications Ortega might suggest, because in the light of his previous criticisms it is intrinsic to the parliamentary system that it will be filled with second-rate people. He does, however, find his way to suggesting certain reforms. As a preface to these, it is worth noting a comment he made in July 1922: 'It is very possible – more possible than the abstractionists of democracy might suppose – that at some moment the necessity for a dictatorship will impose itself, not only in Spain, but also in France, Italy and Germany' (OC 11, 23). One is, I think, entitled to ask why the 'necessity' of dictatorship referred to in this grimly prophetic statement. Some nine months into the dictatorship of Primo de Rivera, Ortega answers this question in the following way: 'political ideas and public affairs have become so complex that the body of society lies scattered in innumerable directions' (OC 11, 34). The fact is, he says, that Parliament cannot cope with such diversity and complexity because 'Parliament is an apparatus invented more for defence and criticism than for construction' (*ibid.*). On this reading, Parliament has proved itself incapable of dealing with the demands of modern society, and therefore ought not to have the prestige which the 'abstractionists of democracy' accord it. In the previous chapter we saw how Ortega massaged socialism into an ideology of national construction, jettisoning much of what is intrinsic to it along the way. Here he is performing the same operation on parliamentary democracy. Notions of participation in such a system are simply not important when placed alongside the task of creating – of 'constructing' – a modern Spain. Everything of value is represented by that end, and at times it seems as though Ortega is prepared to justify any means to achieve it: hence the possible 'necessity' for a dictatorship.

Further ammunition against democracy is provided by Ortega's development around the beginning of the 1920s of the idea that the Spanish people as a whole were as much to blame as their leaders for the failure of their country to make it to the front rank of industrial nations. By 1924, for example, he rejects the traditional analysis of *caciquismo*[1] as a system imposed against the will of the people, in favour of the claim that the will of the people actually contributed to its survival: 'If all the *caciques* were hung tomorrow, who do you think would effectively hold power in the village, the province and the nation in two years' time? I suspect that the reply . . . would be unanimous: in two years' time in the village, the province and the nation the *caciques* would be in charge' (OC 11, 43). And he concludes, 'it is not only the *caciques* who are to blame for *caciquismo*, but also those who have been "caciqued" (*caciquados*)' (*ibid.*).

This rather jaundiced view of public opinion leads Ortega to suggest that if anything useful is to be done with the country, then the first thing would be to ignore such opinion: 'The dictator, like the democrat, if he wants to achieve anything worthwhile, will have to go against public opinion. If not, public opinion will return to what it created: the "old politics" ' (OC 11, 31). Whether Ortega is

[1] See p. 18, n. 2.

correct in this analysis is not a question to be resolved here. What is true, though, is that by criticising the parliamentary system as incompetent, arguing that the complexity of modern society is not susceptible to parliamentary management and questioning the worth of public opinion, Ortega has provided three significant justifications for the suspension of democracy. I am not arguing that Ortega made a direct contribution to either Primo's or Franco's dictatorship with these remarks, but they were certainly sentiments of which retrospective use was made. Once again, the desire to get something *done* in Spain led to the occasional sacrifice of principles which, elsewhere, he defended.

Parliament

These reflections on the inadequacy of parliamentary democracy were accompanied by a sense that the parliamentary system could not simply be abandoned: 'One cannot govern with Parliament, but it is impossible to govern without it' (OC 11, 34). During the dictatorship of Primo de Rivera Ortega pondered at length on the form that such a Parliament should take. What he comes up with is something like a separation of powers. Parliament cannot govern, he says, so what is required is a government, and he recommends a 'parliamentary government' in which Parliament would 'nominate those who were to govern' (OC 11, 37). Once nominated, he continues, the government should be as independent of Parliament as possible, and should be guaranteed a certain (unspecified by Ortega) lifespan because, 'it is not possible seriously to govern when one is at the mercy of the ups and downs of parliamentary rule' (OC 11, 37–8). Sovereignty and government are two different things, he maintains, and a sovereign parliament which attempts to govern will fail in the attempt.

This inevitable failure damages the prestige of Parliament in the eyes of the population at large, and it is the intention of Ortega's proposed reforms to restore its tarnished image. He says: 'The new Parliament ought to meet infrequently and with great solemnity. It ought to debate few issues, but ones of great importance. It ought to maintain a clear distance from what is insignificant and trivial' (OC 11, 40). A further point he makes is that four hundred Members of Parliament is too many, on the grounds that proper discussion is impossible among so many people. He believes that the large number of members in most legislatures is due to the mistaken attempt to approximate to direct democracy, and says that such an enterprise is absurd because people in local districts have no idea of national politics, and so to charge those people with responsibility for choosing national politicians is an error. His recommendation in 1924 is that the 400 members should be reduced to 200, all chosen by regional assemblies – say twenty for each one (OC 11, 46). Why 200 people should find it any easier to have meaningful discussions than 400 is not clear, and indeed Ortega himself (by 1926) has decided that 'ninety or a hundred' would be the optimum figure. The general theme running through this constitutional reform, however, is clear: Ortega believed that the parliamentary system as traditionally conceived was incapable of delivering the strong government which Spain needed for its modernisation. The removal of the direct link between the individual voter and national politics was intended to obviate the danger of the 'ignorant' vote, and to guarantee the competence of those sitting in the legislative chamber. The independence of the executive from the legislature was to ensure the possibility of firm government, with the former free from the irritating, debilitating scrutiny of the latter.

Ortega and John Stuart Mill

These reflections on the reform of Parliament have taken us some way from liberalism. They constitute another example of the way in which two nodal points of Ortega's political thought come into conflict: the desire to see a modernised Spain, and the requirement of a society in which all individuals have a guaranteed, inviolable private space – the former implies control, the latter, the lack of it.

In this context it is curious that his proposals for parliamentary reform, aimed at achieving strong government, should have been conceived at the same time as *La rebelión de las masas*, a book which can be described without distortion as extolling the values of the meritocratic type of liberalism to be found in some parts of John Stuart Mill. Stuart Hall has said of the latter that 'he worried most about the danger of despotic government, the overgrown state, the tyranny of the ignorant majority and the rule of mediocrity' (Donald and Hall, 1986: 60). On this reading, Ortega's concerns in *La rebelión de las masas* are identical with those of Mill, and provide us with another relatively familiar landmark for orientation.

Traditional liberalism may have implied universal democracy, but it never *was* universal democracy, and Mill's reluctance to drink of such a heady brew is matched by Ortega's. Indeed, this reluctance has the same source in both thinkers: a fear of the 'collective mediocrity' of the masses (*On Liberty*, p. 124). 'The general tendency of things throughout the world,' says Mill, 'is to render mediocrity the ascendant power among mankind', and that 'At present individuals are lost in the crowd' (*ibid.* p. 123). Ortega's sentiment is very similar: 'nowadays . . . to be different is indecent. The mass crushes everything that is different, distinguished, individual, eminent and exclusive. Whoever is not like everyone else, whoever does not think like everyone else, runs the risk of being eliminated' (*Rebelión*: 58).

Both Mill and Ortega found themselves living in historical conditions which put their liberalism under pressure. The key elements were the rise of mass society and the demands of the working class for liberalism to make good its promises – the fact of Mill writing in 1859 and Ortega in 1930 is consistent with the lag in Spain's industrial development. How did they react? They could have taken on board Tom Paine's perspective of a truly universal liberalism, but instead they opted for a meritocratic form of the doctrine which was suspicious of democracy and stressed the value of selected individuals rather than all individuals. We will deal with this latter point more fully later in the book, but it should not escape notice that aspects of Ortega's theory of elites are paraphrased by Mill in *On Liberty*. He says that society should 'cultivate individuality', and in reply to the question: what sort of individuality? he refers to those who 'set the example of more enlightened conduct', and remarks, 'these few are the salt of the earth; without them, human life would become a stagnant pool' (p. 122). In this way, Mill opens the door to an elitism which Ortega makes a central feature of his social and political thought. Neither Mill nor Ortega would have found their way to these sentiments had it not been for their living in the shadow of three specific phenomena: the ideology of liberalism, the rise of mass society, and the associated demands of the working class. The possible responses to these phenomena were various, but both thinkers – and Ortega in particular – opted for a meritocratic form of liberalism.

Conclusion

As the classic ideology of the 'bourgeois class aspiring to be the leading class' (Donald and Hall, 1986: 49), liberalism clearly had its historical attractions for Ortega. The various aspects of the role played by liberalism in shaking up British society during the eighteenth century so that the bourgeois class could then mould it in its own image, would all curry favour with Ortega: opposition to the arbitrary power of monarchs; suspicion of the established church; the favouring of an 'open' meritocratic society; the encouragement of 'free thinking'; and the stress on individualism.

Ortega clearly did not believe, however, that Spain's problems were susceptible to classic liberal solutions – at least not on their own. The modernisation of Spain required, as he saw it, a collective effort which the individualism of liberalism could not hope to generate, and it is the tension between these two principles which informs much of his thinking about liberalism and democracy. He does not produce a definitive view of either principle, apparently content to oscillate between meritocratic liberalism and state intervention on the one hand, and support for democracy or its suspension on the other. It would be an error, however, to see these tensions as inconsistencies, because I believe that the best way to view them is in the context of Ortega's overriding concern to see a modern, competitive, competent and united Spain. To this end he is as happy to ransack the cupboard of liberal thought as he is to manipulate the language of socialism.

4

Conservatism and elitism

Ortega's lack of enthusiasm for the Conservative Party in Spain, whether it was run by Cánovas or any of his successors, was total. This is not to claim that he never made conservative-sounding remarks, but that if he did, it was not because he was in favour of the conservatism of the Conservative Party, but because certain of conservatism's central features – such as its anti-utopianism – appealed to him.

Conservatism, generally speaking, has to do with the notion of gradual change, which in turn derives from a characterisation of the human being as embedded in present circumstances which are irremediably rooted in the past, and which circumscribe our potential for action. The conservative frame of mind is past- rather than future-orientated.

Ortega's general insistence is upon the human being as an active, forward-thinking creature, but the stress which he places on the activity of the human being has its limits – limits which are derived from its circumstance. It is clear that his analysis of the relation between me and my circumstance is going to put him at odds with any form of utopian creationism. We cannot create solutions out of thin air because we are irrevocably committed to acting within a certain framework which is constituted by our circumstance. This is the full meaning of a remark which has already been commented upon: 'The only thing which *ought to be* is that which can be, and the only thing which *can be* is that which is already developing within what is' (OC 3, 101). It is when entertaining ideas based on this kind of thinking that he comes closest to operating from within a conservative tradition.

At times he makes his anti-utopianism explicit: 'This is the great correction which our age is going to make to the political ideas of the nineteenth century – the correction from which all others will

72

flow. Because in the nineteenth century almost all political ideas and emotions (progressive as well as reactionary) were, precisely, utopian' (OC 11, 62). This refusal to deal in abstractions is what informs Ortega's cavalier treatment of democracy, as demonstrated in chapter 3. His criticism of the 'abstractionists of democracy' is based on the assertion that future ideals should be weighed against present needs and circumstances, and if the former are found wanting in the light of the latter, then there should be a readiness to abandon them. This kind of pragmatism is typically held to be the preserve of the ideology of conservatism.

Ortega expresses the belief that what is important to the present is the foundation provided by the past, and that attempts at wholesale destruction of the past will result in distortion of the present. At one point, he mentions the 'conservative sociologist' (generically speaking) who would say that even if institutions do not perform perfectly all the time, they may still have a part to play in the political system – their very existence indicates that they have a part to play. Ortega agrees: 'It seems that nature's plan is organised in such a way that we need a certain amount of rigidity and firmness to survive' (OC 10, 390). When contemplating reform, the foundations provided by the past should not be perfunctorily cast aside for it is they that provide the 'rigidity and firmness' on which to base the present. Edmund Burke, widely recognised as the 'father of English conservatism', provides a classic statement of the claims of the past upon the present:

The very idea of the fabrication of a new government, is enough to fill us with disgust and horror. We wished at the period of the Revolution, and do now wish, to derive all we possess as *an inheritance from our forefathers*. Upon that body and stock of inheritance we have taken care not to inoculate any cyon alien to the nature of the original plant. All the reformations we have hitherto made, have proceeded upon the principle of the reference to antiquity; and I hope, nay I am persuaded, that all those which possibly may be made hereafter, will be carefully formed upon analogical precedent, authority, and example. (Burke: 117)

The fear of 'fabrication', the favouring of 'inheritance' and the organic language are all typical of anti-utopian statements, and they are all to be found lurking in Ortega's political thought. The parallels between Burke and Ortega are highly instructive in that the various aspects of Burke's thought which find an echo in Ortega point to an enduring conservatism in the latter's position.

For example, it is typical of both that they refuse to deal in mechanical, geometrical or mathematical terms when making political prescriptions. They prefer to use organic language when talking of human beings, their constitutions and institutions. Burke puts it like this:

I am afraid I have gone too far into their way of considering the formation of a constitution. They have much, but bad, metaphysics; much, but bad, geometry; much, but false proportionate arithmetic; but if it were all as exact as metaphysics, geometry, and arithmetic ought to be, and if their schemes were perfectly consistent in all their parts, it would make only a more fair and sightly vision. It is remarkable, that in a great arrangement of mankind, not one reference whatsoever is to be found to anything moral or anything politic; nothing that relates to the concerns, the actions, the passions, the interests of men.   (Burke: 296–7)

Ortega is equally disdainful of reducing human beings and their enterprises to ciphers and makes frequent use of organic metaphors to illustrate that the 'drawing-board' type of change favoured by utopian social engineers is bound for failure and frustration: 'Abuses [against the nation] are never, never more than localised illnesses which can be fought by the remaining healthy parts of the organism' (OC 1, 274).

Again, both Burke and Ortega are aware that change does, and must, take place. There are times, says the latter, when political institutions seem 'decayed, if not completely rotten' (OC 10, 390), and to this extent he makes it clear that his 'political realism' does not mean 'idolatry to things which have been accomplished and a refusal to modify that which already exists' (OC 11, 63). But, says Burke, 'To make every thing the reverse of what they have been is quite as easy as to destroy', while, 'At once to preserve and to reform is quite another thing' (p. 280). One suspects that he would have agreed with Ortega's solution to this conundrum: 'that we extract the ideal, not subjectively from our heads, but objectively from the things themselves' (OC 11, 64).

The way in which a thinker conceives of political change and how it is to come about is generally illustrative of their political thought as a whole. Ortega's anti-utopianism, his refusal to indulge in 'drawing-board' strategies for change and his insistence on deriving what ought to be from what is, mark off enduring conservative elements in his thought. None of which is to say that Ortega was a conservative – in the context of early twentieth-century Spain he clearly was not. The point is merely that his anti-constructionism placed him in opposition to the wholesale changes demanded by the radical left in general, and the strategy of revolution in particular.

Change, elites and masses

Indeed, enough has been said to know that his opposition to what he called the 'old politics' was total, and that change of some sort was essential to Spain's recovery. Moreover, he had a clear picture of how that change was to come about and who was to instigate it. Consideration of these questions will lead us to the heart of his theory of elites.

While considering his attitude to democracy in the last chapter, it was demonstrated that Ortega entertained a very jaundiced view of public opinion. It is not simply that public opinion is worthless in terms of determining social policy, and that democracy must therefore be called into question as a means of arriving at such a policy, but that the bankruptcy of public opinion makes the existence of a 'moral' elite essential to the health of a polity: 'The people does not think: that part of it which could serve as a brain is precisely that which we call the *elite*, aristocracy, the few, and which we are accustomed to isolate with such care from the many, the common herd (*el vulgo*), the *dēmos*' (OC 10, 64). The historical mission of the elite in this context is clear: 'The people, the many without the few, without the cultured minority, is not capable of accomplishing any historical task worthy of mention' (OC 10, 129). Ortega had in his possession a French 1906 edition of the *Communist Manifesto*. At one point in the manifesto Marx and Engels remark that 'All social movements up to the present day have been brought about by minorities or for the profit of minorities. The proletarian movement is the spontaneous movement of the immense majority in the interests of the immense majority.' Ortega underlined the second sentence with a red crayon and placed an exclamation mark beside it. Bearing in mind his belief that the 'many without the few is not capable of accomplishing any historical task worthy of mention', one can see why. The average man has no historical mission beyond that of drinking from the fountain provided by the select, the few, the elite.

Having identified the historical mission with which Ortega entrusts the elite, we must now ask ourselves who or what this elite is. There is an understandable tendency to think of the words 'mass' and 'elite' in purely numerical terms. They clearly have a numerical sense, and Ortega gives us good cause to follow it through when he provides us, in *La rebelión de las masas*, with 'the datum on which this essay took wing and which, as I said, contains the seeds of all these meditations. From the fifth century AD until 1800, Europe never had a population bigger than 180 million people. Between 1800 and 1914, this population grew to more than 460 million' (OC 4, 215). Similarly, in what is probably the best-known quote from *La rebelión*, he says that,

The cities are full of people. The houses are full of tenants. The hotels are full of guests. The trains are full of travellers. The cafés are full of clients. The pavements are full of passers-by. The waiting-rooms of famous doctors are full of ill patients. Shows – at least those which are relatively modern – are full of spectators. The beaches are full of bathers. That which used to be no problem is now becoming a practically continuous one: finding space.   (OC 4, 143–4)

What often passes unnoticed, however, is that Ortega then proceeds to introduce a rider to this numerical description of the masses. Just a page later he notes that in the past fifteen years (i.e. since the end of the First World War) it is not so much the numbers that have changed – he claims they have stayed relatively stable – but the places where those numbers are to be seen. They are now to be observed 'in the best places, the relatively refined creations of human culture, which used to be reserved for small groups – in short, for minorities'. This point is essential to an understanding of what the revolt of the masses is all about, in Ortega's view. It is not simply that the masses have become involved in things which used to be the preserve of an elite, such as politics, or are now to be found in places which used to be reserved for the elite, such as the waiting-rooms of famous doctors, but that the masses (comprising the 'average man') are simply incapable of handling this world of the elites which Ortega feels they have invaded. On this reading, there are certain aspects of human existence to which only an elite ought to have access: the incursion of the masses into these aspects has done great damage to Western society. We shall return to this point shortly – it is enough for now to recognise that it is not the numerical element of the mass's rebellion which is so crucial, but rather the character of the territory it has invaded.

Ortega is keen to disabuse us of the idea that the term 'mass' has any of the class connotations which we might normally ascribe it:

'Minorities are individuals or groups of individuals who are especially qualified. The mass is that collection of people who are not especially qualified. By masses, then, one should not only or mainly understand 'the working masses'. Mass is 'the average man'. In this way what was merely quantity – the crowd – is changed into a qualitative determination' (OC 4, 145).

Mass, then, has as much to do with the quality of human beings as with their numbers, and, according to Ortega, rather less to do with social class. He does, however, hedge his bets on this issue. For instance, he says at one point in *España invertebrada* that 'In every class, and in every group which does not suffer from serious anomalies, there is always a common mass and an outstanding minority' (OC 3, 103). He then proceeds to qualify this statement: 'Of course it is true that within a healthy society the superior classes, if they really are superior, will be able to count on a better-nourished and more select minority than the lower classes' (*ibid.*). A similar qualification is to be found in the following quotation from *La rebelión de las masas*:

The division of society into masses and outstanding minorities is not, therefore, a division into classes of society, but into classes of men. It cannot correspond to the hierarchy of upper and lower classes. Of course it is true that in the superior classes – when they manage to *be* superior and while they really were superior – there is a greater likelihood of coming across men who adopt the 'great vehicle' [Mahayana], while the lower classes are generally constituted by individuals without quality.

(OC 4, 146–7)

I think it has to be accepted that there is an element of confusion in Ortega on this topic – it simply is not clear whether there is a legitimate social class component in his concept of the elite or not: he has it both ways. Left at that, the point is not particularly interesting, but if we ask ourselves why Ortega makes contradictory statements about what ought to be an important distinction, we come across some data which constitute vital clues as to what he considers the elite to be.

At one point he says, when talking of the elite, that 'Nothing could be further from my mind, then, when talking about the aristocracy, than to refer to that which – through slackness – is usually meant by the word' (OC 3, 103). This is an important qualification for him to make because he often uses the word 'aristocracy' as a shorthand for 'select minority', and he has already made it clear that he wants no social class connotations to be attached to the latter term. Elsewhere, however, he refers to the aristocrat as the 'man without a function' (*hombre sin oficio*) (OC 11, 109), who has plenty of time and space to do as he will. In itself this definition has no specific class content, but a surfeit of time and space was clearly characteristic of the lifestyle of that social class whom we have come to call the aristocracy. To this extent, Ortega's use of the word 'aristocracy' to describe his elite is highly significant.

It is his belief that the elite is composed of people who adopt the widest possible perspective from which to view events. Further, he believes that such breadth of vision is only available to a certain group of people – a group largely defined by what they do. The 'man without a function' will have the time and space to expand his perspective on the world, while the worker, with his nose to the grindstone, will be able to see (literally and figuratively) nothing but the grindstone. These considerations are based on the very foundations of Ortega's conception of the human condition, the details of which will be presented in Part III. For now, the point can be made clearer with the following remarks:

It is hardly surprising that the humble labourer, submerged by his work on the land, or the worker tied to his workshop, or the small businessman, behind his counter, lack the synthetic visions in which the legion of social facts are defined. Neither in Spain nor in any other country does the great collective mass reach self-consciousness. For this reason it is and eternally will be absolutely necessary for any social body to count on the existence of a small number of clear heads where the reflection which the mass lacks can take place. The sad case of our people is that that conscious minority seems not to exist.   (OC 10, 437)

To the extent that the development of that which is characteristic of the elite (synthetic vision) is dictated by a style of life, there will clearly be a social component to Ortega's elite. This is the reason why he makes contradictory statements as to how far his elite corresponds to the social elite – his definition of the elite means that, to a certain extent, it will; while it also implies that it need not. His use of the word 'aristocracy' to refer to the select minority is intended, then, to retain those features of the lifestyle – time and space – of what we normally understand by the aristocracy, while jettisoning its specific class connotations. The new aristocracy, he tells us, comprises 'writers, artists, doctors, engineers – the intellectual class' which indulges in the 'reflection' which characterises the elite.

There is one further distinction between the mass and the elite of which Ortega makes use and to which we ought to refer, a distinction which first appears, as far as I am aware, in *La rebelión de las masas*. He says:

For me, nobility is synonymous with an enterprising life which always aims to overcome itself, to transcend that which it already is towards that which it poses for itself as a duty and a demand. In this way, the noble life stands against the common and passive life which statically shuts itself up, condemned to permanent immanence so long as no exterior force obliges it to come out of itself. In this way we use the word mass to describe that mode of existence – not so much because it is numerous, but because it is passive. (OC 4, 183)

This existential-sounding characterisation of the mass and the elite, according to which the latter 'demands more of itself than the rest' (OC 4, 146), is related to Ortega's conception of life as essentially an affair of choosing:

Instead of imposing one trajectory upon us, [the world] imposes several and, consequently, it forces us . . . to choose. What a surprising condition that is of our lives! To live is to feel oneself *fatally* obliged to exercise one's freedom, to decide what we are going to be in this world. Not for one moment is our activity of decision-making allowed to rest. Even when in desperation we abandon ourselves to whatever is going to happen, we have decided not to decide. (OC 4, 170–1)

In Ortega's terms it is characteristic of the elite that they take seriously this future co-ordinate of human existence. In being self-demanding they 'transcend that which they already are' and move toward the future and are thus living what existentialists would have called an 'authentic' life, a notion in Ortega which will be dealt with later.

These reflections enable us to conclude that Ortega's elite is, first, small in number; second, that its members are to be recognised by the breadth of vision they bring to bear on the world; third, that in principle elite members are to be found in all walks of life; but that fourth, the second point makes it likely that some social occupations are more favourable with respect to the generation of an elite than others – in this way, a social feature is introduced into Ortega's elite conception through the back door.

In historical and political terms, the relationship between the elite and the mass is crucial. The argument is first presented in detail in *España invertebrada* when Ortega asks himself why there are 'no men', by which he means no *select* men. Echoing his argument that *caciquismo* was at least as much the fault of the general public as of the *caciques* themselves, he says that the reason why there are 'no men' is that there is 'no mass', and that this is because 'The social value of the men who guide is dependent upon the capacity for enthusiasm which the mass possesses' (OC 3, 92). Enthusiasm for what? Ortega supplies the answer with a statement which anticipates a theme of his *La deshumanización del arte*:

The sharper, wiser and more profound a writer is, the greater the distance between his ideas and the ideas of the common crowd, and the more difficult their assimilation by the public. Only when the common reader has faith in the writer and recognises his great superiority, will he make the necessary effort to raise himself to the level of comprehension. In a country where the mass, faced with something or someone superior, is incapable of humility, enthusiasm and adoration, it is highly probable that the only influential writers will be the most common ones – that is to say, the ones who are most easily assimilated; that is to say, the most utterly stupid ones.   (OC 3, 91)

The attitudes of the mass towards the elite, then, in a healthy polity, will be one of 'humility, enthusiasm and adoration'. The unhealthy polity, on the other hand, will be characterised by a mass which thinks it can be an elite, which thinks it can invade the territory of the elite without doing damage to the social whole. This is the point of Ortega's remark that it is not the mass itself which constitutes the danger to civilisation, but where it puts itself – in places tradition-ally created by, and reserved for, the elite.

In this context in the *La rebelión de las masas*, he says that mass-man threatens civilisation by thinking that it is something natural, something that does not have to be worked at, whereas in reality it was something 'founded', with much difficulty, by a few people. Mass-man, as a historical phenomenon, has been 'born into' civilisation, as it were, and so conceives of it as natural rather than artificial. Things are only made worse by the increasing complexity of society, which has meant that fewer and fewer people can under-stand it and care for it – all the more ridiculous, and dangerous, then, that mass-man should feel himself capable of running it (OC 4, 199–201).

Ortega's sociology of elitism provides him with a structure which underlies any given political/institutional arrangement a country might have. He says that 'A nation is an organised human mass, structured by a small number of select individuals' (OC 3, 93). Further, he makes the strong claim that this structuring has the status of a natural law: 'It is a question of an inescapable natural law which plays a similar role in the biology of societies to that of the law of densities in physics' (*ibid.*). Natural laws are, of course, impossible to break, and any attempt by human beings to do so can only end in failure or worse: 'When the mass of a nation refuses to be a mass – that is, to follow the guiding minority – the nation dissolves, society breaks up and social chaos and historical invertebration ensue' (*ibid.*). The elite and the mass correspond to two modes of being: 'exemplariness' (*ejemplaridad*) and 'obedience' (*docilidad*), and from this, says Ortega, 'We derive the basic creative mechanism of every society: the exemplariness of the few articulated in the obedience of the many' (OC 3, 104). In *España invertebrada* he is already talking about the 'sentimental revolt of the masses' (OC 3, 125), which he characterises as 'hatred towards those who are best', and expresses the opinion that the condition for Spain's recovery is the recognition of the following: that '*the mass has no mission other than to follow those who are best*' (OC 3, 126; Ortega's emphasis).

Full-blown egalitarianism, then, for Ortega, is ruled out by the existence of a natural law which states that societies will always be composed of a minority and a mass. Societies will be healthy provided their masses are humble and their minorities fulfil their guiding function. Societies will succumb to chaos, however, if their masses refuse to behave like a mass. Hierarchy is not simply a political prescription, it is a *sine qua non* for a society to work properly, and it is vital that everyone within that hierarchy perform the function allotted to them.

In this context, it is essential that the mass recognises itself as mass, and does not believe itself capable of coping with the concerns of the elite. A symptom of modern society, as Ortega saw it, was that the mass was not obeying the law of hierarchy, and that something was required to give it back its sense of 'massness'. One of his best-known books, *La deshumanización del arte*, amounts to a description of the 'new art' as performing just such a function: 'In my opinion, the characteristic of the new art "from a sociological point of view", is that it divides the public into the following two sets of people: those who understand it, and those who do not understand it' (OC 3, 355). The usefulness of this, from Ortega's point of view, is that the new art forces those who do not understand it to recognise themselves as inferior to those who do, as well as causing the select few to consider themselves select. This recognition is the first stage in the re-establishment of the hierarchy he believes to be essential to a healthy society:

For a century and a half the 'people', the mass, have sought to be the whole of society. The music of Stravinsky or the plays of Pirandello have the sociological usefulness of obliging them to recognise themselves for what they are, as 'only the people', a mere ingredient, among others, of the social structure, the passive material of the historical process, a secondary factor in the spiritual cosmos. On the other hand, the young art contributes, too, to the 'best' coming to know each other and recognise each other in the grey mass of the crowd, and to their getting acquainted with their mission, which consists in being few and having to fight against the many.   (*ibid.*)

'Dehumanised' art is art which cannot be appreciated by being lived, but rather has to be contemplated (OC 3, 368). Putting someone in front of a piece of abstract art and observing their reaction will, according to Ortega, tell you whether he or she is a member of the elite or the mass. Abstract art can only be confronted by contemplation, and to the extent that the ability to contemplate is characteristic of the select few, the appreciation – or not – of an abstract work is the litmus test of elite membership.

To summarise, we see that the mass/elite relationship, from Ortega's point of view, is a societal fact of life, and that the consequences of kicking against it are akin to those attendant upon trying to break a law of nature – potentially disastrous. It is the duty of the mass to follow the few whose duty it is, in turn, to provide guidance for the mass. Ortega's analysis of the decay of Spanish society is based on his belief that the mass has come to believe itself capable of being the elite, and he thinks that in the new art he has discovered a means by which the sense of mass and elite will be reasserted.

History, elites and masses

As well as having political and sociological dimensions, Ortega's concept of the elite also provides him with a tool for historical analysis, and it is most fully applied in this context in *España invertebrada*. His starting-point is that, historically speaking, Spain has lacked the guiding minorities necessary for a healthy society: 'While the history of France and England is a history made principally by minorities, it is the mass which has done everything here, either directly or through its representatives in public, political or ecclesiastical power' (OC 3, 110). The gravity of Spain's difficulties, in Ortega's opinion, is demonstrated by the fact that its roots lie not in the nineteenth century, nor even in the national demise which followed upon the glories of the sixteenth century, but back at the time of the fall of the Roman Empire. He notes that it was the Visigoths who found their way to Spain in the greatest numbers in the sixth century AD and who proceeded to dominate the Iberian peninsula for the best part of 200 years.

Ortega claims that by the time they reached Spain they were already 'wasted and degenerate' (OC 3, 117) after their 130-year journey from the Carpathian mountains through what are now Bulgaria, Greece, Albania, Yugoslavia, Italy (to Rome), and along the Mediterranean coast of France. Worse still, in Ortega's opinion, was the fact that 'they had no select minority' (*ibid.*), unlike the Franks who settled in Northern France.

Consequently it is 'the absence of a select minority, sufficient in both quantity and quality' (OC 3, 119) which is the historical fact Ortega seeks to underline, and through which he aims to 'explain' the depth and gravity of his Spain's contemporary difficulties: 'The key to Spain's great problems lies in the Middle Ages' (*ibid.*). He adds that the sixteenth-century 'Golden Age' of Spanish history was, in historical terms, an aberration brought about by the 'unification of the peninsula' which gave strength to the nation while the rest of Europe was still indulging in parochial squabbles. This, though, turned out to be an 'injection of artificial abundance' rather than a 'symptom of vital (*vital*) authority' (OC 3, 120), the proof of which is that the decline began around 1600 and has continued ever since.

Ortega's wide-ranging, if insubstantial, analysis led him to suggest that Spain's was a historical, rather than a political problem, and therefore required solutions of a historical, rather than a political, order. Moreover, having identified the seed of the historical problem in the lack of a guiding minority, Ortega's proposed solution lay in the resurrection of such a minority and, as we have seen, this presupposed the suppression of the revolt of the masses so as to ensure the hierarchy essential to the proper functioning of the mass/elite dynamic. It is all of this that is at the root of Ortega's statements that Spain's problems were historical rather than political.

Ortega and other elite theories

By way of concluding this chapter on Ortega's conservatism and elite theory, it is helpful to place him in the context of other elite theories of his time, for it is important to note that far from being some deranged dream, the idea already had a respectable pedigree by the time Ortega came upon it.

The last quarter of the nineteenth century was the beginning of the era of 'political science', in which writers and researchers hoped to apply the methods of pure science (particularly physics) to the realm of politics in the hope of finding out how it 'really' worked. The most important aspects of a political system, on this reading, were not exhausted by its written constitution (for example), but rather lay in what went on behind the constitution. Following this line of investigation, one of the discoveries made, in Geraint Parry's words, was that there was 'a tendency for control of parties to fall into the hands of a combination of parliamentary leaders and party bureaucrats' (1976: 19). On this basis a whole range of elite theories were advanced by people such as Vilfredo Pareto, Gaetano Mosca and Robert Michels.

Interestingly in our context, Parry also notes the following context for these theories: 'Students of politics were with one breath relating the advent of the mass into politics – were discovering 'the crowd' – and with the next breath were saying that power had never been more restricted to a narrow few' (1976: 20). Similarly, Tom Bottomore comments upon the popularity of elite theories in countries where feudal influence was still strong, and where the concept of hierarchy had therefore hardly begun to be undermined (1968: 15), Georg Lukács has remarked that elite theories have traditionally been developed within countries where no bourgeois democracy has ever taken root and where the feudal frame of mind remains dominant. In this context he mentions Weber's notion of 'charisma' and Pareto's 'elites' – to which we might reasonably add Ortega's 'select few'. That Ortega should make such extensive use of the elite concept is not so surprising, then, in view of the typical social background it enjoyed.

How far he was influenced by the theories of Mosca, Michels *et al.*, however, is hard to say. As far as I am aware he never mentions any other theorist by name, although he clearly read Michels because he owned a 1911 edition of Michels' *Zur Soziologie des*

Parteiwesens in der Modern Demokratie. The only other extant book from his library on this subject is G. Bousquet's *Précis de sociologie d'après Vilfredo Pareto*.

Ortega was much keener on deriving an explicitly prescriptive programme from his theory of elites than other elite theorists have been. His analysis of the mass/elite dynamic as a fundamental law-like feature of any human society led him to make normative proposals such as those encapsulated in his 'Old and new politics' speech, and the Liga de educación política initiative. A further difference between Ortega's position and that of the more 'academic' elite theorists was their respective views on who or what constituted the elite. Most of the latter confined their elite to the political realm. Only Pareto allows for elites in all walks of life, from judges to train-robbers, but he too concentrates, in practice, almost exclusively on the political elite. Ortega's one reference to elite theories other than his own is revealing in this context:

A crude sociology, born by spontaneous generation, and which for some time has dominated the opinions which are going around, distorts these concepts of the mass and the select minority. By the former it understands the ensemble of economically inferior classes – the rabble – and by the latter it understands the higher social classes. As long as we do not correct this *quid pro quo* we shall never advance one step in our understanding of social affairs. (OC 3, 103)

Ortega's point is that there is an elite in all classes and walks of life. Regardless of the detailed differences between his and others' conceptions, however, enough has been said to indicate that the former's theory was not some idiosyncratic aberration, but was rather one species of a genus of socio-political thought common to countries at a similar stage of development to his own, and which have since acquired a respectable academic pedigree. In the final analysis, the similarities between the theories are more instructive than their differences:

All elite theories are founded on two basic assumptions: first, that the masses are inherently incompetent, and second, that they are, at best pliable, inert stuff or, at worst, aroused, unruly creatures possessing an insatiable proclivity to undermine both culture and liberty. The indispens-ability of a dominant, creative elite is, of course, a corollary assumption basic to the philosophy of elitism. (Bachrach, 1972: 2)

5

Nacionalización and decentralisation

Enough has been said by now to lend support to the contention that Ortega's overriding social aim was the modernisation of Spain. We have observed two of the political implications of such a project: the massaging of the language of socialism in the service of national construction, and the cavalier treatment – when necessary – of the principles of liberalism and democracy. Now it is time to analyse the effect of the specifically national focus of Ortega's enterprise, because it provides us with a theme which runs right down through his political thought. It should be noted, incidentally, that this theme places him firmly in the tradition of the Generation of 1898, for whom the recovery of Spain (as a nation) took precedence over all other political undertakings. To the extent that he was locked into this tradition, the national focus of Ortega's concerns obscured other problematic features of the politics of early twentieth century Spain – such as the class struggle which necessarily accompanied industrialisation. From a national perspective, the division of the nation into classes could only endanger the unity required for Spain's recuperation.

This carving-up of the nation into classes is just one example of the 'social illness' (OC 11, 17) which Ortega calls 'particularism' and from which he believed Spain to be suffering 'acutely' (*ibid.*). Again it should be pointed out that this notion formed a part of Ortega's political thought practically from the beginning. His most consistent exploration of the phenomenon of particularism is to be found in *España invertebrada* where it is elevated to the following status: 'particularism is what I call this phenomenon of historical life, and if someone were to ask me what term best captures the character of present-day Spain, I would answer with that word' (OC 3, 67). He continues: 'Today, Spain is a series of watertight compartments rather than a nation' (OC 3, 74). His position

86

is that the institutions and groups in Spanish society – social classes, the Church, regions demanding autonomy, the army – were behaving in ways designed to maximise the satisfaction of their own interests, rather than in the interests of the nation as a whole. This is where his advocacy of the sense of community in socialism, his criticism of the exaggerated individualism in some forms of liberalism, and his successive disappointments at attempts at government by both civilian and military administrations all come together. His reactions to political phenomena of all types were invariably underpinned by the desire for national unity in the task of the construction of Spain, and the accompanying criticism of any manifestations of 'particularism' which might endanger that unity.

'Nacionalización'

If particularism is the illness from which Spain is suffering, in Ortega's opinion, then *nacionalización* is the antidote. In the conclusion to his 'Old and new politics' speech of 1914, for example, he talks of the '*nacionalización* of the army, *nacionalización* of the monarchy, *nacionalización* of the clergy. . . *nacionalización* of the worker' (OC 1, 299). The word *nacionalización*, as Ortega uses it, is untranslatable in English. It can mean 'nationalisation' in the economic sense to which we are most accustomed, but this is not his meaning. He is at pains to stress that it has nothing to do, either, with what he understands by nationalism: 'It must not be thought that the word national, which I have used often in my speech, has anything to do with nationalism. Nationalism supposes the desire of one nation to impose itself on others, which, in turn, presupposes that that nation is at least alive.' And he continues, 'Our aim is very different. As the prospectus of our society makes clear [the prospectus for the League for Political Education], we would be as ashamed to want an Imperial Spain as not to want a Spain in good health. We want nothing more than a vertebrate, upright Spain' (OC 1, 300).

It seems clear that Ortega recognised the danger that his position would be taken as one of an aggressive form of nationalism and was concerned to emphasise that his programme for Spain's revival did not involve imperial designs on neighbouring countries. To be sure, he wanted to see Spain united, but not at the cost of organising its people around an aggressive foreign policy. *Nacionalización* is, in sum, a communitarian notion intended to convey the sense of the integration of groups and interests which Ortega considered crucial to Spain's well-being. It is an expression of his desire that all of the factions in Spanish politics put aside their divisions and organise themselves around a common theme – the revival of Spain.

Similarly, Ortega never defines the nation in terms of blood or race. He says explicitly in *La rebelión de las masas* that a sense of nationhood has nothing to do with factors such as blood, language, or natural frontiers (*Rebelión*: 248), and his assertion here that it is a 'peculiar Western instinct' (*ibid.*) is characteristic of the rather metaphysical foundations on which he builds it. At times he refers to the founding of a nation in terms of a sense of history – 'A people is its mythology' (OC 1, 416) – but more frequently he defines it with regard to the future: 'What is essential for the existence of a nation is not the past, traditional habits, what happened yesterday . . . Nations are formed and nourished by having a programme for tomorrow' (OC 3, 56–7). Similarly, 'A nation is not primarily the past; it is not history and tradition. A nation is the common job which has to be done . . . it is a task' (OC 10, 440). This future dimension of Ortega's definition of the nation is once again best seen, I think, in the context of the projection which dominates his political thought – the construction of Spain. It is evident that such a project will never be fulfilled simply by reference to past glories: indeed the only thing that will get *nacionalización* off the ground, from Ortega's point of view, is the organisation of the various feuding groups in Spanish society around the common task that is the building of Spain's future.

It is in this light that his reactions to regimes such as that of the *Juntas de defensa*, Maura's National Government of 1918, Primo de Rivera's dictatorship, and the Second Republic itself, must be seen. His support for these governments decreased in proportion to his judgement as to the decline in their national, as opposed to particularist, integrity. The typical anatomy of his reaction to a change in the political climate was initial enthusiasm followed by criticism on the grounds of particularism, followed in turn by rejection and the search for a new alternative. I think it fair to say that, for Ortega, a government stood or fell according to its readiness to abandon the particular interests it represented in favour of the interests of the nation.

Ortega's call for *nacionalización* provides another angle from which to view his rejection of the idea of the class struggle, which was noted in chapter 2.

His insistence on the primacy of the nation was bound to cause him to criticise the phenomenon of factions warring within it. This, in turn, led him into inevitable conflict with class struggle as a central tenet of socialism as conceived by the Spanish Socialist Party. Comments such as the following can only be fully understood within this context: 'We do not happen to separate the workers' question from the national question' (OC 1, 303). This sentiment, similar to those seen expressed in the chapter 2, is illustrative of the overriding importance not simply of the nation, in Ortega's political thought, but the historical project of the resuscitation of the Spanish nation during the first third of the twentieth century. Anyone wanting to make sense of Ortega's politics would do well to make this concrete historical context a constant point of reference.

The problem of uniting the various factions of Spanish society around the task of rebuilding Spain led Ortega to refer to Parliament as an ideal type of institution: 'The *Cortes* is the national institution *par excellence*, because in it, the countless particularisms see themselves as compelled to face each other, to limit themselves, to be tamed and to be nationalised (*nacionalizarse*)' (OC 11, 17). This should not, I think, be taken as a necessarily democratic statement of support for the institution of Parliament. In chapter 3 we came across Ortega's view that the parliamentary principle should not stand in abstract isolation, but should rather be dependent upon other contingent political requirements. In this context, his support for Parliament will be conditional upon it delivering the goods; i.e. providing a forum for the generation of national unity.

He leaves us in no doubt that the interests of the nation should come before the interests of anything, or anybody, else – a position based on the firm belief that what is good for the nation is, in any case, good for everything, and everybody, else. In March 1925, for example he talks of liberty, republicanism and monarchism, and goes on to say that, 'Before these three things is the nation: the only essential thing' (OC 11, 54). Similarly, he demands the adoption of a 'national politics', claiming that the problems of the nation are 'more urgent' than those of, for example, political liberty (OC 11, 61). With remarks such as these Ortega is clearly treading the top of a slippery slope. I have no doubt that the step of subordinating liberty and democracy to the interests of a 'vital nation' (*nación vital*) was taken in the best possible faith – his unhappiness at the lack of freedom under both Primo and Franco confirms his belief that there was such a thing as an unacceptable exchange rate. But the truth is that his remarks constitute an intellectual justification for the burying of democratic rights in the dung-heap of the 'national interest'. That some people (such as José Antonio Primo de Rivera) should make unscrupulous use of these ideas is perhaps not surprising; whether it was what Ortega intended is something to be considered in the next chapter.

Nacionalización, then, is a political prescription intended to bury factionalism and promote national unity. I think it is worth pointing out the utopian nature of this project, if only in the context of Ortega's own criticism of utopianism, discussed in the last chapter. If 'what ought to be' has to derive from 'what is', then it is hard to see how Ortega could seriously entertain the idea of a united Spanish nation in the face of the factions – political, regional, generational – present in Spanish society.

More pertinently, it is hard to see such unity existing without it being, in some sense, forced. At times, indeed, Ortega's language verges on the coercive: 'All the institutions of State have to be nationalised because they are all denationalised. By denationalisation I used to understand, and I still do, the fact that this or that institution or organ of the State does not wholly submit itself to the destiny of the nation – to the overriding, historical expediencies of the Spanish nation' (OC 11, 271). Although this stringency could be interpreted unfavourably, I think it more accurate in the context of Ortega's work as a whole to emphasise the liberal mechanism by which *nacionalización* is to come about. The idea is to 'respect the public life of one's enemy (whoever he is), not to begrudge him anything, nor to call into question his rights as a Spaniard, nor to bury them in complexity: the monk and the atheist, the soldier and the civilian and the civilian and the soldier, the employer and the worker and the worker and the employer' (OC 11, 273). This call for the toleration of the lamb by the wolf is both, I suggest, characteristic of Ortega's general position on the question of the generation of unity, and illustrative of the utopian nature of the project. He had, however, left the way open for the adoption of the end (national unity) without the inconvenience of worrying unduly about the means.

Decentralisation

It would be unfair, though, to leave discussion of Ortega's utopianism at that. He was well aware that the disintegration of Spain was not only social but also geographical – both generally in the sense of its size, and particularly, in the sense of the demands for autonomy emanating from Catalonia and the Basque Country. He paid rather more detailed attention to this problem than he did to the question of social unity, and the constitutional reform he derived from his conclusions has not received the attention it deserves.

In the book which captures the essence of this reform, *La redención de las provincias*, Ortega says that, 'The difficulty of turning Spain into a nation is its extreme localism' (OC 11, 242). As early as 1917, however, he saw that something positive could be extracted from the difficulty. Referring to the bankruptcy of the old political bandwagons such as liberalism, conservatism and radicalism, and the absence of any clear alternatives for the future, Ortega says: 'Between that past which is vanishing and this future which has not yet come, there is an obvious attitude for all serious Spaniards to take up: the organisation and affirmation of local life' (OC 10, 375). And in the same article he hints at a theme which is to be everpresent in his work on this subject: that of the sense of purpose which can be engendered by people having responsibility for their own lives: 'It is necessary that the humblest corners of Spain learn to feel the proud desire to be themselves, that they be the protagonists of their own lives, and not the scorned and silent flocks of extras which moves in a line at the back of the stage' (OC 10, 376).

Very soon, this kind of comment comes to occupy a central place in Ortega's political strategy, particularly from around the end of 1918 when he is searching for solutions after the failure of Maura's National Government. He says: 'A glance at the national scene shows that there are only two organic nuclei of political potentiality: the decentralisers and the groups of those who work' (OC 10, 453). And, two days later, he goes on: 'The only concrete, definite and extensive project which now exists in the public mind with regard to what that other, better Spain – which is longed for from the Bidasoa to the Mediterranean – ought to be like, is decentralisation' (OC 10, 455). From this point on, Ortega's reflections on the issue of decentralisation become more frequent and more complex, culminating in the writing of most of *La redención de las provincias* in article form between November 1927 and February 1928, and its publication in March 1931. This chronology, together with the mention made above of the gestation of the idea around 1917 or 1918, gives some idea of the time he devoted to it and the seriousness with which he regarded it, and also indicates his frame of mind at the advent of the Republic. All the more reason, then, to wonder at the lack of attention this has received compared to his 'nationalism', 'corporatism', 'fascism', or call it what one will. The fact that this aspect of Ortega's thought has been ignored has led to some very misleading remarks being made, such as the following from John Butt: 'His [Ortega's] politics later evolved, but there is no doubt that in the 1920s he was still under the influence of the extreme right-wing theories he had learnt from his German professors' (1978:20). Apart from creating the mystery of Ortega's 'right-wing professors' (the two most inflential of his German professors were both social democrats), Butt's contention fails to take into account the goodly proportion of Ortega's work during the 1920s devoted to the issue of decentralisation and the fostering of political responsibility – themes which, taken together, can hardly be called 'extreme right-wing'.

Three main features of his notion of decentralisation ought to be pointed out. In the first place it satisfied his demand that political solutions should not be utopian but rather should be rooted in the circumstances already existing. Second, he saw it as a means of fostering a sense of responsibility in the 'average Spaniard'; and third, he felt that it would contribute towards restoring the tattered prestige of Parliament. This last is because Parliament's involvement in local affairs detracted from its ability to deal with the national work for which it was designed, and which it is most competent to undertake. Ortega's conclusion for the balance of responsibilities is as follows:

I imagine Spain having a new anatomy, with the Peninsula organised into large regions. Each one would be governed by a Regional Assembly or Local Parliament, which would appoint its executive magistrates. The Assembly would be composed of delegates elected by direct universal suffrage according to constituencies. This local Power would be charged with dealing with all the issues arising within the province. Central Power and its national Parliament would be left very few issues, i.e. strictly national problems and functions, including the right to intervene in the regions when one of them is suffering from an anomalous situation.(OC 11, 88)

This last phrase may seem like the small print which calls the rest of the document into question, but I do not think that this is Ortega's intention. As we shall see later, his aim is to ensure that the centrifugal forces of such an arrangement do not cause the whole apparatus to fly apart – I think it fair to say that he would envisage the 'intervention clause' being invoked very sparingly. National government would control 'only the Army, Justice, a part of communications, international life, the right to intervene in the affairs of local government and the constant option to establish regulatory services in the fields of teaching, science and the economy throughout the peninsula' (*ibid.*).

There is an approximate equivalence between these ideas and the Constitution drawn up by the Founding Fathers of what was to become the United States of America, at least in terms of the considerable powers given to local government. The difference, I think, is of degree rather than of type – it is not clear exactly how much influence central government would have over regional government in Ortega's scheme, whereas the American Constitution guarantees the states certain freedoms from federal interference. What is clear is that he thought that the centrifugal tendencies in Spanish regionalist politics could be best dealt with within the framework of a dispersion of political power rather than its central concentration. A unitary solution to the problem, then, along the lines of the British political system, was never on his agenda.

It may seem curious that such an implacable advocate of the cause of a unified and upright Spain should spend so much time on the issue of devolving power to the regions. The first point to be made in this regard is that he did not conceive of the regions as having more than a minimal influence on national policy: the general direction in which the country was to go would be decided solely by national government. Secondly, he believed that the devolution of responsibility to the regions rather than to the municipalities would encourage the development of a wider political perspective in the general population. The individual would become used to placing the necessities of the municipality in the wider context of the necessities of the region, and from there it would be a small step to taking into account the interests of the nation as a whole. Third, he thought, as we have seen, that a Parliament freed from dealing with regional questions would have more space to develop a responsible, unequivocal national policy: one which would be so sensible that no regional government could fail to see its wisdom.

Conclusion

It is hard to conclude a chapter on the themes of *nacionalización* and decentralisation when what appears to be two opposing tendencies are defended with equal vigour by the same person. As I have indicated, the link between the two, in a territorial sense at least, is provided by the belief that decentralisation will generate widespread public, political responsibility, which will be reflected in a commitment to the wider polity (i.e. the nation) beyond the claims of particular interests.

The contributions Ortega made to the Catalan question during the first year of the Second Republic amount to an attempt to put these ideas into political practice. The attempt foundered on the rock of the radicalism of Catalan demands, and Ortega's belief that internal demands for autonomy had to be seen in the same light as the loss of Spain's colonies – as a symptom of the collapse of the nation. Unity could only be preserved by acknowledging the dominance of the Spanish state and its cultural symbols – such as the Castilian language. Ortega therefore found himself painted into a corner, defending precisely the type of Spanish nationalism he always hoped to avoid. His last word on the issue of particularism in general, made in December 1933 when he had ostensibly 'retired' from politics, is revealing:

That politics which plagues us and which serves the interests of groups, classes, and regions [*comarcas*][1] is precisely the politics which has failed throughout the world. One after the other, partial interests – capitalist, pro-worker, militarist and federalist – have abused the state once they have taken control of it, and the abuses have ended up cancelling each other out, leaving the way clear for the affirmation of moral values based on the idea of the Nation. (OC 11, 530)

The content of the message is the same as it ever was – only the form is different. His exasperation at both the failure of the liberal mechanisms he had hoped would engender *nacionalización*, and at the intransigence of regional interests in the face of his proposals for decentralisation, is evident. Only the shell of the idea – the Nation – is left, and others were to make unscrupulous use of it.

---

[1] Ortega's *comarcas* would be Galicia, Asturias, Castilla la Vieja, País Vasconavarro, Aragón, Cataluña, Levante, Andalucía, Extremadura, and Castilla la Nueva.

6

Fascism?

Ortega has often been accused of making a direct contribution to Spanish fascism, generally in its falangist rather than its Francoist guise. This chapter is an attempt to set limits on the scale of this contribution. One or two points should be remembered throughout. The first is that history is replete with figures who have been dragooned (often posthumously) into causes which it is hard to imagine them having supported. In the context of fascism, Hegel and Nietzsche are two names which immediately come to mind. I think it is generally recognised that to call these two fascist thinkers is to stress some aspects of their thought out of all proportion, and to ignore others entirely, as well as to make the mistake of an ahistorical analysis: fascism was not a nineteenth-century phenomenon. Another example of an even more ludicrous nature is provided by Karl Popper's assertion that Plato somehow had something to do with the modern totalitarian state, and this brings me on to the second point which ought to be borne in mind.

The word 'fascism' (like the word 'totalitarian') has become a term of abuse which tends to be thrown around whenever it is felt that there are political points to be scored. This has two effects. First, 'fascism', in true Humpty Dumpty style, comes to mean practically whatever one wants it to mean, and second, the actual content of the thought of whoever it is that is being called a fascist becomes distorted by the label applied to it. Similarly, it will not have escaped notice that the blanket-term 'fascist' has a chalk-and-cheese quality: it is generally used when the moral and political issues at stake are seen to be clear-cut, when 'good' and 'bad' are easily and clearly recognisable.

The Spanish Civil War and the subsequent Franco regime were, of course, perfectly suited to such Manichean interpretations: you were either for Franco or against him, for the Republicans or against

95

them – there could be no middle way. In this kind of atmosphere, sensitivity to the nuances of a person's thought is hardly likely to be at a premium. Once that person has been identified with a particular side in the battle between 'good' and 'evil', everything that he or she says or does will be interpreted in the light of that battle, and inconvenient contrary evidence will simply be ignored. This, I believe, has been Ortega's fate.

During the long struggle against Franco there was neither time nor need for sophisticated analysis. What was required was a method for the rapid determination of sympathies, and the fact that the founder of the Falange, José Antonio Primo de Rivera, for example, expressed an intellectual debt to Ortega was enough to condemn the latter to the ranks of fascism for the duration of the dictatorship – and beyond. This conclusion was reached at the cost of reading history backwards – by reading Franco back into Ortega's work. In this book we have been reading history forwards, and enough has been said already to see that Franco and Ortega, and even José Antonio and Ortega, would have been argumentative bedfellows. Only now, with the dictatorship receding into the past, is it possible to write a fuller account of the relationship between Ortega and fascism. The final point to be made is that there is no smoke without fire, and that I think it best to begin the chapter with a look at the features of Ortega's thought which lend themselves to accusations of fascism.

Language

First, one ought to note the organic nature of his political language. This is a features shared by both conservatism and fascism to the extent that they constitute a reaction against Enlightenment rationalism and mechanicism, and the stress on the organic community stands in opposition to political theories based on individualism. Ortega, for example, says that, 'Spain is a social organism: it is, so to speak, a historical animal' (OC 3, 111). He talks of the 'biology of societies' (OC 3, 93) and of the people as a 'body' (OC 1, 512). He talks of the 'vitality of societies' and refers to the Crusades as 'marvellous examples of a profusion of vitality, of superabundant energy, of sublime historical sport' (OC 3, 118).

In this context, it ought to be noted that Ortega's *razón vital*, in so far as it involves an assessment of the limitations of pure reason as an instrument for understanding the world, has been seen as a form of irrationalism by some commentators, and has thus provided fodder for those keen to find fascism in Ortega. I say that this is a simplistic interpretation of his position, but justification of that must wait until the final section of the book. I will say, however, that it is arguable that not only have interpretations of his politics suffered from the Manicheism of the Franco period, but that so has his philosophy. Political rejection by the left has resulted in philosophical rejection by 'progressive' commentators who might find something there if only they would look. Nevertheless, the point is taken that the organicist, biological language habitually used by Ortega to describe the polity is more firmly in the conservative/fascist tradition than any other.

The nation

Ortega has a tendency to be prepared to sacrifice means to ends, as was seen in the context of his treatment of democracy in an earlier chapter. This lack of principle in itself is clearly open to cavalier use by the unscrupulous, but when the end to which the means are to be sacrificed is the nation, loud alarm bells begin to ring. Ortega is perfectly happy to place the nation above the institutions of the state: 'Let us try to make the Spanish nation turn its back on the Spanish State, as if on an unfaithful servant. The functions of the State must cease to be of such importance' (OC 10, 280). Written in 1915, these words could constitute a justification for the suspension of the Cortes by General Primo de Rivera, the Nationalist uprising in 1936, and any amount of cynical misuse of the state's institutions during Franco's dictatorship. This disrespect for the gains made by liberal democracy is captured in the following statement: 'Every democratic man, that is to say, every man who respects the idea of law, ought to prefer to see legality suspended than to see it mocked and ridiculed' (OC 10, 628).

Similarly, when particularly depressed at developments in Spain during the years of the *trienio bolchevique*, he sometimes went for short-cuts which made a mockery of the democratic rule of law of which he was generally in favour: 'Give Power to Caesarists or Bolsheviks, but let the men who are chosen have an air worthy of their responsibilities' (OC 10, 638). And he continues: 'the first thing that has to be done is, precisely, to restore social authority, and it can be white, red or blue, just so long as it exists' (*ibid.*).

This stress on authority, without regard for the recipes of the people who are to wield it, will clearly seem irresponsible to those who think means to be as important as ends, and who believe that there should be ways of ensuring that authority is justly exercised. We are already familiar with Ortega's attack on the disease of 'particularism', and in this context it is the nation which provides the idea to which distinct interests ought to submit: 'This is very simple: the nation is the point of view in which collective life is integrated above and beyond the partial interests of classes, groups or individuals' (OC 11, 413). The implications of Ortega's desire to bury particularism could be far-reaching in political and institutional terms: there is clearly room, for example, for Mussolini's 'corporations'. At the Italian Fascist Trade Union Congress of 1922, it was proclaimed that, 'The Nation, understood as the supreme synthesis of all the material and spiritual values of the race, stands above individuals, categories and classes, which . . . are not legitimate unless they are contained within the framework of the superior national interest' (quoted in Carsten, 1970: 74). Again, the principles of the *sindicatos verticales*, or vertical trade unions, of the Falange in Spain were based on the need to co-opt workers and management into a structure which would undermine the class struggle in favour of the transcendent interests of the nation. One has no difficulty, then, in seeing that Ortega's war against particularism and his stress on the overriding importance of the nation, amounts to a corporatism which became a tributary of fascist theory and practice.

The limits of Ortega's national project should, however, be emphasised. In a previous chapter one saw him, in 1914, going out of his way to play down the aggressive interpretations which might be made of the idea, and even in 1930, while proposing the founding of a 'national party', he says, 'A national party is a party which points inwards towards the nation, and is therefore exclusive of nationalism which implies confrontation with other nations' (OC 11, 272). I think it fair to say that Ortega never seriously entertained the idea of an aggressive, imperial Spain: his 'nationalism' was confined to the peaceful, internal modernisation of Spain – something which he thought could never happen as long as the body politic remained riven with tensions. It is important to stress this because, on this score at least, it puts him at odds with the autumn 1931 manifesto of the nascent Juntas de Ofensiva Nacional Sindicalista (JONS) which demanded imperialist expansion and the acquisition of Morocco and Algeria (Carsten, 1970: 197). Ortega would never have condoned such a programme.

Practically all the evidence for his aggressive intentions comes from a particularly nasty passage in *España invertebrada* where he expresses the belief that, in a country torn apart by dissensions, force is justified in bringing people together if their prejudices work against 'historical necessity'. He says that, 'Against them, the only effective thing is the power of force, grandiose historical surgery' (OC 3, 57). More inflammatory still, he asserts that victory by force of arms is like passing a historical aptitude test: 'Victory has more of an illustrative than a material effect. It demonstrates the superior quality of the victorious army in which, in turn, the superior historical quality of the people which forged that army appears symbolised and expressed' (OC 3, 58). This looks very similar to General von Bernhardi's sentiment that, 'might gives the right to occupy or to conquer' (in Eccleshall *et al.*, 1985: 224).

Three things ought to be said about Ortega's statement. First, only someone who has read all twelve volumes of his collected works is in a position to say that *España invertebrada* is the only place where such a statement is to be found. It is unique. Second, *España invertebrada* is probably his second most famous book after *La rebelión de las masas*, and as such bears much of the burden of half-informed opinion as to assessments of his political thought. Third, *España invertebrada* was, apparently, José Antonio's favourite book by Ortega. Facts such as this have led many to conclude that Ortega was José Antonio's intellectual mentor. I would go along with this as long as it is remembered that Ortega wrote many, many books and articles besides *España invertebrada*, a good proportion of which would not have appealed to José Antonio in the slightest. Hopefully, enough has already been said to demonstrate the validity of this position.

A further consequence of Ortega's insistence on the supremacy of the interests of the nation was the threat to party political pluralism. From very early on, at least since 1918, he began to insist on the need for a 'social movement' rather than a 'political party' (OC 10, 462–3), and before and during the Republic, especially, his calls for a national party became a constant theme of his political pronouncements: 'it is necessary to get together an enormous nationalising party (*un partido nacionalizador*), above and beyond the 'rights' and 'lefts' which are absurdities inappropriate to this critical moment of European destiny. A huge, overwhelming party, so big and so short on fads and crazes that it could hardly be called a party' (OC 11, 272).

The idea of going 'beyond' left and right is, of course, common to corporatists, falangists and fascists throughout the Europe of the 1920s and 1930s. In June 1931, for example, *La Conquista del Estado* (The Conquest of the State), the newspaper of Ramiro Ledesma Ramos and Onésimo Redondo Ortega, founders of the JONS, ran an article which declared, 'Long live fascist Italy! Long live Soviet Russia! Long live Hitler's Germany! Long live the Spain we shall make! Down with the bourgeois parliamentary democracies!' (Carsten, 1970: 197). Similarly, José Antonio said at the founding of the Falange in October 1933 that 'The movement now founded is not a party, but a movement *per se* – I could almost say an anti-party. It must be stated clearly once and for all that it belongs neither to the right nor the left. The right intends to maintain an economic order that is unjust. The left wants to overthrow the economic order, even if that means losing much that is good' (José Antonio Primo de Rivera, *Obras completas*, 1, 193).

The similarity between this and Ortega's ideas need no stressing. It is important to recognise, however, that Ortega, even when in corporatist mood, never wholly abandons his liberal instincts. There is never, for instance, a suggestion that the 'national movement' should crystallise in the form of dictatorship. In fact, Ortega is continuously and implacably opposed to the principle of one-man rule: 'A dictatorial regime is very dangerous because we believe that it is impossible to avoid the jump from a bloodless dictatorship to one which is fierce and relentless' (OC 10, 510).

As ever, it is important to soothe some of Ortega's isolated remarks with the balm of the wider context of his work. What emerges, I believe, is the picture of someone with liberal pretensions caught up in the historical context of a decline of faith in the ability of liberal democracy to deal with the problems of inter-war Europe. Put this way, the correct balance is achieved, in assessing Ortega's thought, between liberalism and other more corporatist tendencies. It would be surprising *not* to find such tendencies in someone of Ortega's social class writing in Europe in the inter-war years, but that does not make him a fascist, or even a falangist.

Elitism

We have already looked in some detail at the elitism which is so characteristic of Ortega's thought, as well as at the implications for democracy that went with it. This, too, was a feature of some strands of European thought during the first third of the twentieth century, with Pareto, Michels, Mosca (as we have seen) and Nietzsche and Le Bon all offering variants on the themes of fear of democracy and loathing of the masses. Ortega's contribution to this line of thought was hefty, and was inevitably picked up by both opponents and supporters of nascent Spanish fascism. José Antonio, for example, whose *señoritismo* set him apart from the traditional demagogic nature of European fascism, borrowed heavily from Ortega's conception of the elite. His express aim was, 'to select minorities – not many, but few, though ardent and convinced; for so everything in the world has been done' (quoted in Carsten, 1970: 200). The virtual word-for-word similarity between this and some of Ortega's expressions again needs no emphasis.

Fascism

To recapitulate, there is clearly enough in Ortega's language, his favouring of ends above means, his rejection of pluralism in favour of the national interest and his elitism to make him a useful source for fascist or falangist ideologies. Whether this makes him a fascist or a falangist is another matter. A trawl through the concrete statements Ortega made about fascism reveals that the most positive thing he said about it was the following, referring to Italy and Germany: 'There are seeds of inspiration in them, to be made use of, but no more' (OC 11, 421).

Far more common is the sentiment expressed in the following extract from the manifesto of the Agrupación al servicio de la República: 'Fascism and bolshevism are signposts that only direct people to dead ends; therefore, no sooner were they born than they began to suffer from a lack of clear-sightedness'. Why? Because, 'Both forgot that, today more than ever before, a people is a huge historical enterprise which can only be sustained or brought to fruition through the free and enthusiastic collaboration of all its citizens, united by a discipline born of spontaneous fervour rather than of imposed severity' (OC 11, 126).

The call for free association rather than enforced conformity is central to Ortega's rejection of the concrete manifestations of fascism. He may have been asking for the impossible, but he did not seek to make possible the impossible through force, and it is the enduring influence of his humanist liberalism which forever marks him off from the authoritarian cynicism of fascism.

As in the quotation above, Ortega's criticisms of fascism generally double as criticisms of bolshevism. This does not say much for his powers of political analysis, as the class base and economic function of both phenomena are so completely different to defy direct comparison. It ought to be said, too, that he appeared more fearful of bolshevism than of fascism (letter to the Condesa de Yebes, FOC C.199 JK 39/51 11.5.38), but the foundation of his ultimate rejection of both of them is clear: both fascism and bolshevism are, in his opinion, mass, statist movements. It is no coincidence that his attack on Mussolini's fascism is built around an attack on statism:

State intervention leads to the following: the people are converted into meat and drink which feeds the State which is a mere artefact, or machine. The skeleton eats the meat around it. The scaffolding makes itself the owner and tenant of the house. Once this is realised, it is a little disturbing to hear Mussolini preaching, with exemplary vanity, as if the formula: *Everything for the State; nothing outside the State; nothing against the State* were some fantastic discovery made only now in Italy. This alone would be enough to reveal fascism as a typical movement of mass-men. Mussolini found himself with a State admirably constructed – not by him, but by precisely the ideas and forces against which he is fighting: by liberal democracy. He confines himself to using it indecently and, without allowing myself to judge the detail of what he has done, it is unquestionable that the results obtained up to now cannot be compared to the political and administrative achievements of the liberal State. If something has been achieved, it is so insignificant, so invisible and so insubstantial, that it does not balance the accumulation of irregular powers which that machine is allowed to wield in such an extreme fashion.

(*Rebelión*: 182; emphasis in the original)

We have here all we need to see why Ortega could never have gone along with any of the historical manifestations of fascism. This quotation amounts to an encapsulation of the main principles of the *La rebelión de las masas*: a defence of the achievements of liberal democracy (Ortega never suggested that liberalism was at fault in its having 'incubated' socialism, as fascist apologists tended to do); an attack on the 'mass-man'; an attack on excessive state power, and an implicit favouring of individualism (which in Ortega's case means *select* individuals rather than all individuals). *La rebelión de las masas*, which I consider to be much more repesentative of Ortega's political thought than *España invertebrada*, is a definitive statement of his aristocratic, select-individualist liberalism, and as such contains no crumbs of comfort – beyond the theme of hierarchy – for would-be fascist seekers after inspiration. I think, too, that the fact this was also one of José Antonio's favourite books tells us more about José Antonio's aristocratic *señoritismo* than it does about Ortega's pretensions to fascism.

At the end of the day, however, the question 'Was Ortega a fascist?' cannot be satisfactorily resolved here. This is because the question soon disintegrates into several further questions: 'What is fascism?'; 'Do we mean Francoism (what is Francoism)?'; 'Do we mean Falangism (what is Falangism)?', and an introductory book on Ortega has no mandate to tackle these questions. Nevertheless, if it cannot be *satisfactorily* resolved, it can at least be *summarily* resolved by saying 'no', and I think that enough evidence has been produced throughout the book to stand as justification for such a summary conclusion. The most interesting and plausible contention which stands against it is that expressed (for example) by Adolfo Muñoz Alonso in his book on José Antonio, *Un pensador para un pueblo* (A Thinker for a People): 'If I were to be understood aright, I would venture to say that José Antonio sought to bring about in politics the embodiment of Ortega's ideas' (1971: 39). Unfortunately, even the extended treatment that this contention requires is impossible, because it implies an analysis of José Antonio's ideas which are beyond the scope of this book. I would, however, like to point out the lines which such a treatment might take, both because I believe Muñoz Alonso's assessment to be wrong and because so many other people would agree with it.

That there are similarities between the political thought of Ortega and José Antonio is not in dispute – I simply want to maintain that the differences are still more substantial. It is probably fair to say as does Ian Gibson in his *En busca de José Antonio* (In Search of José Antonio), for example, that *España invertebrada* provided the leader of the Falange with a source for his ideas on the unity of Spain (1980: 24–5). Similarly, his criticisms of socialism's internationalism and strategy of class warfare are practically identical to those of Ortega and have the same inspiration – the desire to bury divisiveness in the name of national unity. His doubts about capitalism, too, echo Ortega's assessment of it as materialist and dehumanising.

Where they part company, however, is over the question of the value and values of liberalism. José Antonio is an unrelenting critic of what he sees as the social atomisation which necessarily accompanies liberal politics. Ortega's thought, on the other hand, is characterised by an enduring sense of the value of the individual which does not sit comfortably with the conformity demanded by Falangism and fascism. One could argue, as I have done, that Ortega's defence of the individual is a defence of select individuals – of meritocracy – rather than a defence of all individuals, but the fear of uniformity, of 'mass politics', remains.

A further consequence of Ortega's liberal sensibilities is his cautious treatment of the role of the state in political life. José Antonio's reforming zeal led him to view the state as that which would put right the inequalities fostered by liberalism. Humanity, he says,

wants States which do not only limit themselves to telling us what we can do, but which provides everyone with the means of actually doing it, while protecting the weak and demanding sacrifices, without malice, of the powerful. Two types of State try to achieve such an ambition. One is the socialist State, sound in its starting-point, but barren from then on because of its materialist conception of life and its sense of struggle between classes. The other is a state which aspires to the integration of peoples, in the heat of a common faith. Its name begins with 'f'.   (JA OC 1, 175–6)

José Antonio wants less 'liberal verbiage' and less 'going on about individual rights' (JA OC 1, 193), and in February 1935 he said in a conversation with Unamuno that 'We profoundly respect the dignity of the individual. But I cannot agree to allow the individual harmfully to disturb the common life' (*ibid*. 551). It is these sentiments which ultimately mark him off from Ortega and which call the bluff of Muñoz Alonso's assertion that José Antonio was the embodiment of Ortega's political ideas.

Conclusion

The period between the wars in Europe was not a happy one for liberalism and the political domain was dominated by collectivist movements. In exaggerated terms, any would-be actor in the political arena was confined to two options – socialism (or some version of it) or fascism (or some version of it). Ortega's anti-egalitarianism and sense of hierarchy, coupled with the national focus of his political prescriptions appear to put him in the latter camp, and made him meat and drink to those searching for the foundations of Spanish fascism.

Retrospectively, Ortega clearly contributed to those foundations, but through others' use and interpretation of his work rather than through his own explicit intentions. The fact that Ortega's work was plundered by Spanish fascists does not prove that he was a fascist or even that he approved of any of the manifestations of Spanish fascism. In fact, his absolute refusal to lend his support to either José Antonio Primo de Rivera or to Franco (much to the former's disappointment: see 'Homenaje y reproche a Don José Ortega y Gasset' in JA OC 2, 828–31), is far more indicative of his political orientation than any ideological co-opting that might have taken place.

In the context of a dictatorship such as Franco's, there is likely to be a large gap between what a person believes and what other people, with axes to grind, say that he believes. Only as the dictatorship recedes into the distance is it possible to present a more all-embracing view of Ortega's political thought. What emerges is the picture of a bourgeois, liberal thinker historically, socially and politically squeezed between the demands of an organised working-class and newly fledged corporate solutions to the crisis of capitalism. In the final analysis, it is those features of his thought which would have made him a political companion of the John Stuart Mill found in *On Liberty*, that pull him back from the brink of the abyss of fascism.

III

7

What is philosophy and why is it done?

In February 1929, Ortega began teaching a course at the University of Madrid entitled ¿Qué es filososfía? (*What is Philosophy?*). The course constituted the first complete approximation to his mature philosophy, and it has been suggested – I think correctly – that the catalyst for Ortega's beginning to put his house in order was the appearance in 1927 of Heidegger's *Sein und Zeit* (*Being and Time*). Ortega was surprised and disconcerted to find that Heidegger's book contained ideas similar to those he had been entertaining at least since 1914 in the *Meditaciones del Quijote*, and an allusion to Heidegger in the course of 1929 makes it clear that the German philosopher was a central point of reference: 'To live is to find oneself in the world . . . in a very recent and brilliant book Heidegger has made us take note of the enormous significance of those words' (OC 7, 416). Further: 'I am pleased to recognise that the person who has made most progress in the analysis of life is the new German philosopher Martin Heidegger' (*ibid.*). From 1929 onwards it was Ortega's intention to respond to Heidegger's publication of *Sein und Zeit*, and ¿Qué es filosofía? constitutes his first attempt to formalise ideas which had been gestating for so long.

He begins by asking, 'Why does it occur to man – today, tomorrow or whenever – to philosophise?' (OC 7, 307), and, 'What I would like to do is to take the very activity of philosophy – philosophising itself – and submit it to a radical analysis' (OC 7, 279). He then rehearses Aristotle's answer to the question of why we do philosophy: 'According to him, the origin of knowledge consists in the use of exercise of a faculty which man has, in the same sense in which looking would be no more than the use of vision' (OC 7, 313). In other words, it is the existence of faculties such as memory, and the ability to abstract, infer and compare, which 'make' us do philosophy. We philosophise because we have the tools to do so.

In a course entitled *¿Qué es conocimiento?* [QC] (What is Knowledge?), given in the offices of the *Revista de Occidente* at the end of 1929 and the beginning of 1930, Ortega rejects Aristotle's position on the grounds that the possession of a faculty does not necessarily entail its use (QC, 76). In *En torno a Galileo* (Concerning Galileo), a course of twelve lessons given in 1933 in Madrid's Central University, he makes this point explicit by providing an example: 'It is not good enough to say that because things have being (*ser*) and man has the faculty of discovering it, then it is natural for man to exert this faculty. Chess, also, has pieces and rules, and man has the faculty of moving the former and complying with the latter, but one does not therefore define man as a chess-playing animal' (OC 4, 83–4). So if it is not the fact that we have certain faculties suited to the activity of philosophy which makes us philosophise, why then do we do it? Returning to *¿Qué es filosofía?*, one can see Ortega sketching his answer: 'If man goes to such desperate lengths to use his intellectual abilities, it is not simply because he has them, but, by contrast, because he finds himself lacking something which he needs. In order to secure this something he naturally puts into operation the means he possesses' (OC 7, 314). The activity which we call philosophy, then, is born of necessity. The faculties we possess which make philosophy possible are not, as it were, a luxury, but rather means we use to provide something which we lack.

This notion of a lack is central to Ortega's perspective because it constitutes both the motor of the philosophical enterprise and the key to answering the ontological question posed at the beginning of the chapter. Put differently, the lack or absence which we experience provides the impetus for philosophy, and through an analysis of the origins of the experience of this absence we will 'come across' the radical reality which Ortega is seeking. It should be mentioned that this approach is constitutive of his technique. His intention is not to construct or deduce conclusions from *a priori* propositions, but to take turns around a problem, such as what is philosophy? or what is knowledge? and see what conclusions are arrived at. He describes this approach as the 'Jericho method', and often uses the metaphor of 'stumbling upon' (*tropezar con*) to illustrate the way in which his discoveries are made. In this context, the question: what is philosophy? and the answer given to it, will lead us to the heart of Ortega's philosophical enterprise.

But what is it that we lack, and in what realm is the lack revealed to us? Ortega asserts that it is a feature of the human condition to need completeness: 'everything that is there, whatever is present, given or evident, is essentially a mere piece, slice, fragment or stump. We cannot see it without visualising and feeling a need for the portion that is missing' (OC 7, 330). More explicitly, he quotes Kant: 'When the conditional is given to us, the unconditional is presented as a problem' (OC 7, 333). In other words, the lack that we experience and which moves us to engage our intellectual faculties is the unconditional, the radical – that which 'completes' what is given to us by providing it with a firm foundation. In the wider context of Ortega's philosophy, incidentally, it might fruitfully be suggested that the use of the word 'intellectual' here is misleading. By the end of this section of the book, it will be clear that Ortega suggests that other faculties – apart from those which we might normally call 'intellectual' – can and do play a crucial role in our relating to the world. I would argue, however, that his presentation and proof of what he considers to be basic, or radical, reality is an intellectual one, and that this will become clear in the next chapter. At the same time, he does himself refer to the use of 'intellectual abilities' (as on the previous page), and when he does so he seems to be employing the word in an entirely uncomplicated sense. I propose, therefore, to continue using the word but it may be as well to bear in mind that it represents a potential tension in Ortega's thought.

A statement in *En torno a Galileo* as to how and where we become aware of the necessity for intellectual security provides a concrete indication of the realm in which its lack is experienced: 'It is not the case that man lives, and then, if it comes to it, and if he experiences some special curiosity, becomes involved in forming ideas for himself about things. No: to live is already to find oneself forced to interpret our life' (OC 5, 28). Ortega's position is that philosophy is a consequence of living, in that it is in life that lack, and the necessity of filling it, is experienced. So 'that desire which seems so peculiar to philosophy is simply the natural spontaneous attitude of our mind in life' (OC 7, 310). In this case, it is clear that our experience of a lack is not primarily or initially an intellectual experience – it is rather a pre-intellectual experience which is the result of our being alive. Life is therefore the reality in which philosophy is grounded.

One question which arises here is whether Ortega intends us to take it that we all do philosophy, simply by virtue of being alive. Up until 1933, it is certain that Ortega's answer would have been in the affirmative. In the 1929–30 *¿Qué es filosofía?* he says that philosophy is 'born of life itself' and that 'one cannot avoid philosophising, even if only in an elementary fashion' (OC 7, 317). Again, in a course given in Madrid in 1932–3 entitled *Unas lecciones de metafísica*, he writes that 'the metaphysical undertaking is an unavoidable ingredient of human life' (OC 12, 99), and goes on to assert that everyone has done, and does philosophy, even if it has only been a question of choosing between various interpretations of the world.

Part, at least, of the reason why Ortega can remain content, at least until 1933, with the somewhat surprising assertion that we all do philosophy, is that he allows the word a broad definition. We have already seen him referring to it as the search for a radical reality; the exercise of faculties such as abstraction, inference and comparison; the 'use of intellectual abilities', and the 'choosing between various interpretations of the world'. With such a broad definition, we may well be able to agree that everyone does philosophy, although this does not accord with what we might normally consider to be philosophy: most of the works of Plato, Spinoza's *Ethics*, Kant's *Critique of Pure Reason*, or Wittgenstein's *Tractatus Logico-Philosophicus*. It should be stated, however, that this is not Ortega's last word on the matter. Partly through a tighter definition of the word, partly through historicising the appearance of philosophy, and partly through the development of the idea of 'authentic' thinking, Ortega came to assert that *not* everyone does, or did, philosophy. These changes will be discussed shortly.

What never changes, however, is Ortega's belief that philosophy is a function of life, and this is the point that requires stressing here. In *¿Qué es conocimiento?*, he writes: 'Every question–problem leads us with perfect continuity to an infinity of problems – that is to say, to the awareness that everything is problematic. The reminder that nothing is in itself non-problematic, i.e. that there is no firm ground on which to support oneself, makes us feel *lost in our life* (*vitalmente perdidos*). This is the state of mind which gives birth to philosophy' (QC, 26; my emphasis). From this perspective, the function of philosophy is to provide a firm intellectual base, and its existence is in turn a function of finding oneself alive and thus irrevocably and necessarily committed to interpreting one's life to one's own satisfaction.

Ortega employs a variety of metaphors to illustrate the role that philosophy plays in life. He refers to it, for example, as an attempt to 'touch the bottom', in the sense in which we ask someone in a swimming-pool or in the sea if they can 'touch the bottom': 'We seek a radical orientation with respect to our entire circumstance or, in other words, with respect to everything there is. In order to achieve it we need to satisfy ourselves as to what, in our opinion, there really is, or what is the radical reality. In more commonplace but clearer language: we need to touch bottom' (OC 12, 120). Similarly, he refers to the activity of thinking in terms of swimming to keep afloat: 'thinking is swimming to save ourselves from being lost in chaos' (QC, 156), and in his prologue to Emile Brehier's *History of Philosophy* (1942), he writes: 'Philosophy is swimming so as to float on "the sea of doubt"' (OC 6, 406). José Luis Molinuevo considers that 'the idea of "salvation" – although not entirely original – constitutes the crux of Ortega's philosophy. It gives meaning to the relationship between the I and its circumstance and, given that life is like being shipwrecked, it explains the role of philosophy as knowledge which leads to salvation' (Molinuevo: 10). Philosophy's function within life, then, is to provide intellectual security by constructing a life-saving apparatus – but what does this apparatus look like?

If philosophy is the general activity of saving oneself, then Ortega conceives of the concept of *ser*, or Being, as the instrument one uses to accomplish the rescue. According to him, Being is a concept which human beings have constructed to provide them with something radical and permanent to which to cling, and to this extent is differentiated from things (*cosas*) which have no need of human beings for their existence (this latter point is a simplification of Ortega's position: there will be more to say on it later). In *¿Qué es conocimiento?* Ortega says that 'things or entities comprise that which one encounters, while being or essence comprise that which one looks for' (QC, 71). Given what has gone before, it will be understood that this search for Being has nothing to do with luxury or caprice: it is the result of our being immersed, and disorientated, in our life, and irrevocably committed to interpreting it. Ortega summarises his position like this: 'Things do not in themselves have a being. Being arises from a necessity which man feels with respect to things. What necessity? The following. (We insist on it.) Man is nothing other than life. To live is to find oneself shipwrecked among things. There is nothing one can do apart from grab on to them. But they are fluid, vague and contingent' (QC, 154). So (and this is the kernel of Ortega's interpretation of Being) 'behind the appearance of things as given at any one moment, man constructs the "permanent, changeless thing" – in other words, the Being of things' (QC, 155). On this reading, Being is a concept constructed by us through philosophical reflection so as to provide us with intellectual security. Philosophy is the means by which the concept of Being comes into being, and both philosophy (as activity), and being (as instrument) derive from life, constitutively and definitively conceived as the state of 'being lost', 'shipwrecked' or 'disorientated': 'The truth is that I do not exist because I think, but on the contrary, I think because I exist, because life presents me with basic and inexorable problems' (QC, 150).

This, then, is the outcome of Ortega's submitting the 'very activity of philosophy to a radical analysis'. Philosophy is one of many tasks which human beings undertake. Its practice presupposes the existence of human life and has its origins in it. In his 1940 version of *La razón histórica*, he writes:

Lying behind, and presupposed by, methodical and theoretical doubt, forming an integral part of it and in the final analysis giving it meaning, we find, not the thought of Descartes, but Descartes the man, who finds himself existing in an environment which he does not know, in an atmosphere of darkness and confusion, without being able to fall back on anyone because nobody else has managed to make things clear.

(OC 12, 190)

The radical reality, or the root, of Descartes' existence is not the fact of Descartes thinking, but that primary, pre-intellectual situation which made him think in the first place: his life and the problems it posed. In similar vein he suggests that the physicist cannot avoid this primordial relationship with the world which both presupposes the activity which we call physics, and which poses questions physics cannot answer:

The mission of physics is to work out the principle of every fact or event or, in other words, the antecedent fact or event which gave rise to it. But this principle has, in turn, a previous principle, and so on successively right back to a first, original principle. The physicist renounces the search for this first principle of the Universe, and that is all well and good. But I repeat that the man in which each physicist resides does not renounce it and, either willingly or against his will, finds himself looking for that first and enigmatic cause. It is natural that it should be so. To live is, of course, to deal with the world, to head towards it, to act in it, to occupy oneself with it. It is therefore constitutively impossible, because of a psychological necessity, to renounce the possession of a complete notion of the world, an integral idea of the Universe.   (OC 7, 316)

Earlier, Ortega's belief that philosophy has been, and is, practised by everyone, was briefly discussed. In the light of what has been said since, I suggest that this belief is an intelligible result of his analysis of why we do philosophy: as long as one is alive, it would seem, one is committed to doing philosophy, or at least something like it. It was further noted that this was not Ortega's last word on the subject, and that three factors caused him to modify the assertion. One of these factors – the historicisation of the activity of philosophy – will now be considered. As far as one can see, the change took place around the middle of 1933, but the interest of this is not only biographical – it also bears substantially on Ortega's mature opinion as to what philosophy is and why we (or some of us) engage in it.

In August 1934, Ortega wrote a letter to the Condesa de Yebes in which he said that he had been involved in 'two years of intense meditation' (FOG C. 199 JK 36/51 28.8.34). Counting back, this would mean that both *¿Qué es filosofía?* and *¿Qué es conocimiento?* (the two courses on which we have concentrated so far) predate the period of meditation. But what was it that he was meditating on?

In one of a series of articles entitled *Guillermo Dilthey y la idea de la vida* (Wilhelm Dilthey and the idea of life), published in the *Revista de Occidente* in November, December and January of 1933 and 1934, Ortega wrote the following: 'I knew nothing of Dilthey's philosophical work until four years ago. I had no adequate conception of it until the last few months. I would say that this ignorance has made me lose approximately ten years of my life – that is to say, ten years of intellectual development. But this of course implies an equivalent loss in other dimensions' (OC 6, 170). Ortega's own chronology suggests, then, that he felt that he had made reasonable assimilation of Dilthey's work by the middle of 1933. This is the first clue to the subject of Ortega's two years of meditation. It would, I might add, have been hard for him to reach an earlier assimilation because the German edition of Dilthey's collected works which he read was not published until 1927–31. Similarly, in the articles referred to above, he mentions three other factors which prevented him from an earlier acquaintance with Dilthey.

First, Ortega arrived in Berlin in 1906, by which time Dilthey had stopped giving public lectures and had surrounded himself with a small coterie of specially prepared students; second, one could not obtain a copy of Dilthey's *An Introduction to Human Studies* because it was 'one of the rarest books on the market'; and third, the book was always out of the library when he wanted it (OC 6, 171–2). I suspect that these difficulties would not have been insurmountable had Ortega had a genuine interest in Dilthey at the time, and he would surely have been able to remedy them at a later date had he so wished. This debate is, however, beyond the scope of the present book – it is my intention solely to establish when Ortega did feel he had effectively assimilated Dilthey, and to illustrate the importance of that event.

In this context, it is of more than passing interest that of all the books in Ortega's private library (open to the public in the Fundación Ortega y Gasset in Madrid) the collected works of Dilthey are the most heavily annotated – far more than those of other philosophers to whom he makes reference in his work, such as Kant and Leibniz. The bulk of these annotations, and the sustained work they represent, would seem to have been made after 1931 (the date of publication of the last annotated volume of Dilthey's collected works). This circumstantial evidence lends further credence to the suggestion that Dilthey was the subject of Ortega's two years of meditation between 1932 and 1934.

Now, if we take Ortega's chronology at face value and accept that he only achieved a thorough acquaintance with Dilthey in the middle of 1933, then not only *¿Qué es filosofía?* and *¿Qué es conocimiento?*, but also *Unas lecciones de metafísica* are to be placed before the period of meditation referred to in his letter to the Condesa. From our perspective, the importance of this is that most of the ahistorical references to the practice of philosophy are to be found in these three courses, and that from now on, Ortega is clearly intent on giving that practice a concrete historical content. My point is that a conception of philosophy which places its practice within a particular period of time *ipso facto* means that not everyone has always done it. The historicisation of philosophy places a temporal limit on such practice. This is the change that a reading of Dilthey forced upon Ortega.

For it was indeed *history* that Dilthey taught him. In *Origen y epílogo de la filosofía*, Ortega wrote that Dilthey 'taught us more radically than any of his predecessors – Hegel, Comte – to see historicity as a constitutive feature of the human being' (OC 9, 396). It should be noted in passing that Ortega's recurring criticism of Dilthey was that the latter conceived of philosophy as one of the 'permanent possibilities of man' (together with religion and poetry). Ortega expresses surprise at this because of Dilthey's insistence on historicising phenomena in the human world, but this is rather unfair in the light of his position as expressed in this chapter. In *¿Qué es filosofía?*, *¿Qué es conocimiento?* and *Unas lecciones de metafísica* (i.e. between 1929 and 1933), Ortega advances the view that philosophy is not only a permanent possibility for man, but actually a permanent necessity.

Nevertheless, from this time onwards, Ortega's answers to the questions of what philosophy is and why we do it come to contain a historical moment. The framework within which he operates is developed in *Ideas y creencias* (Ideas and Beliefs), originally conceived as the first chapter of a book he never completed and which was to be entitled *Aurora de la razón histórica* (Dawn of historical reason). *Ideas y creencias* was written around December 1934.

The technical meaning Ortega intends for 'belief' is expressed in the following way: beliefs 'are not ideas which we have, they are ideas which we are'. And, 'properly speaking, we do not *do* anything with beliefs, we are simply *in* them' (OC 4, 384). Beliefs provide a foundation on which we depend for picking our way through life. Ortega writes that most people, most of the time, are not aware of what their beliefs are. His description of our relationship with our beliefs gives rise to another technical term – he writes that we 'count on them (*contar con ellas*), without pause' (OC 4, 386); and defines the content of 'counting on' in the following way: 'the manner in which something intervenes in our life without our thinking about it, I call 'counting on it'. And this is the manner proper to our active, or effective, beliefs' (OC 4, 387).

The beliefs of which Ortega writes are never individual, in the sense of being idiosyncratically held. They are more akin to notions such as 'the spirit of the times'. Among the examples he gives are belief in God and the belief in reason's capacity to give us knowledge (OC 4, 391). In his 1944 *La razón histórica* Ortega took this latter point further by referring to two different types of mental activity: 'intellectual activity'; and that which produces 'states of drunkenness, delirium, trance and exaltation'. Our belief is that the first type is that which will allow us to 'recognise what reality really is', but 'primitive man . . . believed . . . that it is visionary thought which reveals the most basic reality' (OC 12, 254–6). Both of these are beliefs, in Ortega's technical sense, and it is the first one which is operative in the modern world: we 'count on it' without thinking about it.

Beliefs do not constitute reality – they are interpretations of reality, or ideas about it which have consolidated into beliefs: 'It is important to note that what we usually call the real or "exterior" world is not the naked, authentic and primary reality which man finds before him, but rather is already an interpretation made by him of that reality – in other words, an idea. This idea has consolidated itself into a belief. To believe in an idea is to believe that it is reality, therefore to stop seeing it as an idea' (OC 4, 405–6). Beliefs, then, presuppose the existence of ideas, but some ideas become beliefs, and once they do, our relationship with them changes – we stop 'thinking about' them and begin to 'count on' them. Ideas pass from a stage in which we are aware of them to a stage in which we are not (beliefs), but it is always possible to bring beliefs back into the realm of awareness, although only some people do it, and then only some of the time. It is crucial not to mistake what we believe about reality for reality itself. *Radical* reality is reality previous to any theory about it, and in Ortega's opinion it is the task of philosophy to reveal the nature of that radical reality, and so to provide us with this most basic orientation – i.e. the firmest possible intellectual ground on which to stand.

The implication of this is that there are three possible levels of reflection: thinking about ideas, thinking about beliefs, and thinking about radical reality, with the last being the most fundamental. Thinking about beliefs is, in turn, more basic than thinking about ideas in that it comprises reflection on the very basis of an epoch's intellectual sensibilities. It is the description of a people's beliefs, rather than what they discuss, argue about or die for, which ought to constitute the study of history, writes Ortega (OC 4, 387). Evidently one here has to accept a different understanding of beliefs to that which we are normally accustomed. Beliefs are, in ordinary terms, precisely those sets of ideas which we discuss, argue about and may even die for.

Most important for us, Ortega's position is that *fundamental* thinking only takes place when an epoch begins to lose faith in its beliefs, i.e. when ideas come into conflict with beliefs. These moments of crisis are rare in history, and Ortega's *En torno a Galileo* is dedicated to describing their typology. Moreover, he considered the first third of the twentieth century to represent just such a moment of crisis, with the implication that his thinking was of the fundamental sort described above. In *La idea del principio en Leibniz*, written in 1947 and published posthumously without having been checked by Ortega, he writes, 'Man dedicates himself to that strange occupation which is philosophy when he finds himself lost in his life *because he has lost his traditional beliefs*' (OC 8, 267; my emphasis).

Compare this with earlier statements such as, 'one cannot avoid philosophising, even if only in an elementary fashion' and, 'the metaphysical undertaking is an unavoidable ingredient of human life'. Once a reading of Dilthey forced a consideration of history on Ortega, and once he developed a framework of ideas and beliefs, the activity of philosophy became unavoidable no longer – in fact it now has its origins in a particular moment in time, before which no one had ever done philosophy. In *Origen y epílogo de la filosofía*, Ortega asserts that philosophy 'came about one fine day in Greece' (OC 9, 397), and in his prologue to Brehier he adds that this took place in the 'sixth century BC' (OC 6, 406). Philosophy, then, has its origins at a particular time in a particular place, and to this extent the Ortega of 1934 differs from the Ortega of 1929–33. But the 'structural' reason for philosophy remains the same. In Brehier Ortega continues to use the swimming metaphor, and says that philosophy came about when it did because certain people in Greece in the sixth century BC needed to find 'a new piece of firm ground on which to set foot so as to acquire a new security and foundation' (OC 6, 406), and that this was because they had lost faith in their gods (OC 9, 410 and 422). In other words, it is still the sense of being lost which provides the impetus for the philosophical enterprise. But now first, we are only lost when our beliefs suffer a crisis – under normal conditions our beliefs are what sustain us; and second, Ortega implies that philosophy is not the necessary outcome of this state: other methods of 'touching bottom' could be, and have been, tried – as is to be described very shortly.

This historicisation of the origins of philosophy gives Ortega what he considers to be a reason for criticising Heidegger, particularly in *La idea del principio en Leibniz*. He says: 'Heidegger (who, having started off on the right foot, has come to generate confusion) has got it wrong when he claims that philosophy appears in man when he is *surprised* by the world, when the things around him which he used and which were his equipment (*enseres*) (*Zeugen*) fail him'

(OC 8, 271). Ortega does not agree with this perceived position of Heidegger because, 'man is *a nativitate* surprised by the world . . . but he has not always done philosophy: further – he has hardly ever done it' (*ibid.*). Then, 'This initial mistake leads Heidegger to sustain that man *is* philosophy and that this is because (another mistake) man, when confronted by the failure of the world as an ensemble of *gear* and *equipment* (*enseres y trebejos*), of things-to-use (*cosas-que-sirven*), discovers that these things are alien to him and that they therefore have their own *Being*, which man consists in asking after' (*ibid.*). Ortega's response is that 'It is not true that man has always asked after Being. On the contrary, Being has only been asked after since 480 BC, and then only by a few men in a few places' (*ibid.*). It should be noted in passing that Ortega's use of the date 480 BC here does not square with other chronologies he gives. On the previous page, for example, we saw him talking of the 'sixth century BC' as ushering in the practice of philosophy. I am grateful to Sabina Lovibond for pointing out that this latter date would incorporate the active period of Thales of Miletus and the first pre-Socratics. When Ortega uses the date 480 BC he would seem to be thinking more of Socrates himself (*c.* 470–399 BC). In any case, the fact that he does not appear concerned with consistency indicates that the precise date of the appearance of 'philosophy' is of no great consequence to him.

The thrust of Ortega's criticism of Heidegger, nevertheless, is that he has not gone far enough in his analysis: he has taken the fact of philosophy without taking a historical perspective on the question of why we do it. If he had done so, he would have discovered that *we* (i.e. every people that has been directly influenced by Greek culture since 480 BC) philosophise because we are 'surprised by the world', but that other peoples, also 'surprised by the world' because that is a constitutive feature of all human lives, have responded in different ways. Thus;

The drum is the instrument which symbolises the system of beliefs and norms for very many primitive peoples. And that is because the religious and 'intellectual' activity *par excellence* – that is the relationship with the transcendence which is the world – is the ritual collective dance. This is an extraordinary thing, and it obliges me to suggest to my friend Heidegger that for the blacks of Africa, philosophy[1] is dancing, and not asking after Being.   (OC 8, 287)

---

[1] To avoid misunderstanding here, 'philosophy' should perhaps be in inverted commas, as indeed 'intellectual' is above. Ortega's use of the word in this context is dictated by effect rather than precision. Dancing is not philosophy.

His belief is that philosophy constitutes one 'way of thinking', but that there are other ways of thinking which many people on earth have used and still use: mythological, visionary, shamanistic and so on (OC 8, 287–8). All of these ways of thinking fulfill precisely the same function of providing human beings with firm ground on which to feel 'intellectually' secure. Philosophy remains as a function of life, but it is now, in Ortega's mature opinion, only one solution to the problems posed by living a life and being obliged to interpret it. Philosophy, he says, 'is not a permanent feature of man's existence: it is neither ubiquitous nor timeless. It is born and reborn at determinate moments in history which are characterised by the fact that in them a faith, a collection of "prevailing opinions", or of traditional cognitive conventions, succumb' (OC 8, 293). It was Ortega's further belief that he was 'doing philosophy' *precisely because* he was the judge, jury and executioner of one of these 'traditional cognitive conventions'. This theme will be pursued in the next chapter.

It remains now to clarify one last factor in Ortega's mature thought with respect to the questions of the why and the what of philosophy. Earlier, it was suggested that Ortega's first opinion was that everyone did philosophy, even if only of an unsophisticated sort. One factor has already been mentioned which causes us to revise this impression: the definition of philosophy has been reduced somewhat. First, philosophy is now an activity which has only been undertaken since (approximately) 480 BC, and even since then it has not been a permanent feature of human existence, but has only been carried out when 'prevailing opinions' suffer collapse. Second, there is the implication that philosophy is to be equated with 'asking after Being'; and third, he indicates that this has only been done 'by a few men in a few places'. This last is the factor which deserves attention.

It has been established that philosophy, in Ortega's opinion, is a response to a constitutive feature of life: the sense of disorientation and shipwreck which comes with being thrust into life and obliged to make sense of it. This opinion undergoes some modification in his mature work in that disorientation is reasserted as a permanent possibility, rather than as a permanent fact. In *El hombre y la gente* (*Man and People*), a course prepared by Ortega for the Institute of Humanities (session 1949–50), he says that: 'It is constitutive of man, unlike all other beings, to have the capacity to get lost, to get

lost in the jungle of existence' (OC 7, 99). Similarly, 'The capacity
and the discomfort of feeling lost is man's tragic destiny and his
illustrious privilege' (*ibid.*). The change is small but significant. It is
no longer a necessary feature of the human condition to be lost.
Having the capacity to be lost implies that 'being lost' is not a permanent fact, but a conditional possibility. Furthermore it implies
that, far from being the normal state in which to be, getting lost
actually requires some effort: we have it in our power to get lost, but
we may not necessarily use it. Naturally, what Ortega means by
'getting lost', here, is the sense of being emotionally and intellectually adrift, rather than the way in which everyday objects 'get lost'.

An understanding of this point requires recognising that Ortega's
philosophy here touches his sociology. In *En torno a Galileo* he writes:
'On finding ourselves living, we find ourselves not only among
things, but also among men; not only on the earth, but also in
society. And those men and that society into which we have fallen,
by virtue of being alive, already have an interpretation of life, a
repertory of ideas about the universe, a set of prevailing convictions'
(OC 4, 25). In other words, when we come into the world, we find
philosophies, ideologies and opinions in general about the world
already there, and to this extent we can consider our obligation of interpretation done for us. This acceptance of prevailing convictions
is what Ortega calls 'inauthenticity'. The social world, in general,
is the inauthentic world: 'the social pre-existence of human occupations' constitutes a 'constant invitation to inauthenticity' (OC 6,
403).

On this reading, life still obliges us to orientate ourselves, but
Ortega stresses that there is such a thing as 'fictitious orientation'
which is that which we accept from our 'social surroundings' (OC
12, 30). In *Unas lecciones de metafísica* he continues: 'Enough has been
said to see that man can find himself in one of two situations: an
authentic situation, which implies disorientation and thus obliges us
to try and orientate ourselves; and a fictitious or false situation in
which we imagine ourselves to be orientated' (*ibid.*). Ortega further
explains that one is tempted to lead a 'fictitious life' because the
sense of 'feeling lost' produces 'horror' in us (*ibid.*).

In the specific context of philosophy, by 1942 he is not saying that
everyone does it from necessity, as he held in *¿Qué es filosofía?* and
¿Qué es conocimiento?. On the contrary, he writes that some are,
'attracted to it for inauthentic reasons – that it is a paid profession

and so will provide a daily crust, that it has prestige, or other "purer" but still not authentic motives, such as coming to philosophy because one has a taste or curiosity for it' (OC 6, 403). Those who come to do philosophy for these reasons find it already there; they never think it, individually, for themselves: 'On the other hand, the authentic philosopher who does philosophy for reasons of innermost necessity does not begin with a philosophy already done, but rather he finds himself doing his own, to the point at which the most characteristic thing is to see him bouncing off the philosophy which is already there, rejecting it and retreating into the terrible solitude of his own work' (*ibid.*).

This 'terrible solitude' is increasingly presented in Ortega as being the source of all that is good. The rejection of the social world became ever more radical as his conviction of its representing the realm of the inauthentic, deepened. It is clear, too, that this radical individualism gives his 'meritocratic liberalism' a metaphysical basis. One's plan of action, on Ortega's reading, is only genuinely conceived through a withdrawal into solitude, and nowhere does he transcend this means-orientated expression of plan- and decision-making. The result is that decisions appear to have to be judged by the way that they are arrived at rather than by their consequences for their agents or their peers. To this extent, Ortega's reflections on morality lack the means-orientated dimension that some might consider desirable. As a reviewer for the *Times Literary Supplement* put it, 'I withdraw into my radical solitude, I return with a plan of action. But what if my plan is a plan for tyranny?' (4.3.60, p. 150). This is the type of question which Ortega never addresses: his ethics is implicit rather than explicit and never receives separate or sustained treatment.

Conclusion

In *¿Qué es filosofía?*, *¿Qué es conocimiento?* and most of *Unas lecciones de metafísica* (i.e. from 1929 until 1933), Ortega presents philosophy as being a permanent necessity of the human being. It is described as being one of many activities which human beings undertake and, like those other activities, it has its origins in human life. Life has a variety of features and presents a variety of problems. The feature which gives rise to philosophy is that the human being is thrust into the world and is obliged to make sense of it. More particularly, we are obliged to orientate ourselves in a situation which is constitutively disorientation – i.e. human life. Philosophy is the name we give to that activity which aims to provide us with firm intellectual ground on which to stand. Further, Ortega claims that we, through doing philosophy, have constructed the notion of Being, which represents stability and permanence behind the disturbingly impermanent nature of the things we encounter in the world.

Ortega never rejects the idea that life is the presupposition of philosophy, but the historicisation of the philosophical enterprise leads him to believe that philosophy is only one of many possible responses to the necessity for orientation which life brings with it. Philosophy becomes an activity which has been practised since roughly the sixth or fifth century BC, and which began in Greece, but has rarely been practised since. In the first place, philosophy has only radically been done when the beliefs of an epoch or people encounter ideas which call the beliefs into question. Strictly speaking, in Ortega's opinion philosophy has only been radically carried out on two occasions, once when it began, and once with Descartes. This position will become clearer in the next chapter, while in the conclusion I shall pursue the suggestion that Ortega considered himself and those who thought like him to be the vehicles of philosophy's third authentic moment.

Similarly, the existence of a social world into which we are born, and which already has a repertory of interpretations to offer, represents the temptation to accept the social at the expense of the individual. Inauthentic thinking is that which falls for this temptation and refuses to think individually. Two and two only authentically equal four when the reasons for the equivalence have been individually thought through. The 'man' is authentic and the 'people' are inauthentic, and philosophy can only radically be done by the authentic individual. The question of authenticity will be returned to in the chapter concerning truth.

By submitting the activity of philosophy to analysis, Ortega had demonstrated that it presupposes human life, and that it arises in the context of the intellectual problems posed by life. In the light of subsequent chapters, it will become clear that this 'stumbling upon' life is no accident, but is a function of human life being the radical reality in which all others are rooted and on which they depend. through asking what philosophy is and why it is done, Ortega glimpses human life as the source and foundation of all our activity. In the next chapter this informal expression will take on a formal philosophical character, as Ortega seeks to demonstrate that human life is the radical reality which it is philosophy's task to discover and describe.

8

Idealism, realism and radical reality

Philosophy, for Ortega, is that activity in which some of us engage when we seek intellectual security. Its task is to provide us with the unconditional which lies behind the conditional. The philosopher is faced with the challenge of discovering that reality on which all others depend – what Ortega calls radical reality, or *realidad radical*.

In *¿Qué es filosofía?* and *¿Qué es conocimiento?*, he sets out two conditions that such a principle must fulfill if it is to be truly radical: it must be 'ultimate and integral', or, as he also puts it, 'autonomous and pantonomous'. Thus: 'A truth is ultimate when it does not refer back to or presuppose another. It is integral when it is absolutely true with reference to all other truths, and this is only possible if all other truths refer back to it or presuppose it' (QC, 27). And, 'Because of its unlimited range and the radical problematic of its subject, philosophical thought has to comply with two laws or obligations. It has to be autonomous, in the sense of not admitting any truth which it itself has not generated; and it has to be pantonomous, in the sense of not being definitively content with any position which does not express universal values, or which does not, in other words, aim at the Universe' (OC 7, 349). Finally, 'Philosophy is a science without presuppositions. By this I understand a system of truths which has been built without admitting as a foundation any truth which has been accepted as proved outside of the system' (OC 7, 335).

These two principles provide the check which must be made on any reality which is claimed to be radical, or ultimate, or which claims to be the foundation of all others. It must be suppositionless, and it must take account of all other truths. If it can be shown to make suppositions which come from outside the system, or to leave out of its account truths which other systems have shown to be valid, then it is neither radical nor integral. The reality which Ortega

126

claims to be radical must, then, satisfy both of these conditions.

In the previous chapter, Ortega was presented as 'stumbling upon' life as the presupposition and foundation of philosophy. Philosophy, then, is not sufficient unto itself, but is dependent for its existence on human life which obliges us to interpret it. The aim of this chapter is to demonstrate that, in Ortega's opinion, not only is human life presupposed by philosophy, but also by all other phenomena and realities. I shall follow Ortega's chain of reasoning as rigorously as possible, not only so as to reproduce faithfully the content of his argument, but also so as to illustrate the method by which he arrives at his conclusions. His intention is to avoid imposing assessments on the material – rather he seeks to allow reality to 'reveal itself'. In this context he makes frequent reference to the fact that *alētheia*, the Greek word for truth, means dis- or uncovering. In his opinion, this should be the aim of philosophy – to dis-cover reality, or to 'stumble upon' it.

Throughout Ortega's work, Descartes is presented as dividing the history of philosophy in two: 'Like a gigantic Wall of China [he] divides the history of philosophy into two great halves. The ancients and the medievals are on the other side, while on the side we encounter modernity' (OC 7, 367). Philosophy, it will be remembered, constitutes the search for solidity. Ortega holds that two basic positions have been taken up with respect to the provision of the reality which will provide such security – positions which he generally refers to as realism and idealism. To the extent that he believes Descartes to have ushered in the era of idealism, he (Ortega) identifies Descartes as the dividing line between ancient and medieval responses, on the one hand, and modern responses, on the other, to the problem of insecurity posed by life.

For realism, he writes, radical reality was constituted by 'the world', or 'nature'. Further, realism held that things existed 'in their own right, or for themselves': 'being, in its strictest sense, is independent being, being on its own account or in its own right'. Realism, then, constituted the first response to the need imposed by life to seek the radical reality in which all others are founded. Ortega claims, contentiously, that the second was 'that which Descartes inaugurated and in which we have been educated throughout our lives: that which affirms thought, or the idea as the radical reality – idealism' (OC 12, 170–3). It may seem peculiar to assert that Descartes was the first idealist, but the relevance in our present context of these remarks is that it is Ortega's intention to submit both realism and idealism to examination, to show that neither can claim to have demonstrated what the radical reality is. Finally, through a consideration of idealism in particular, he will show that both theories presuppose another reality, human life, which turns out ultimately and integrally to be the radical reality.

Realism

In *Unas lecciones de metafísica*, Ortega characterises realism as holding that 'reality or being consists in things and their ensemble, which we call world' (OC 12, 104). As noted above, one of the characteristics of 'things' in this context is that they are independent of the observing subject, and a second is that their being is held to be 'static' or 'fixed' (*ibid.*). It should be recognised that Ortega is employing the word 'realism' in its modern sense of the affirmation of the existence of objects independently of their being perceived.

As it happens, he does not dispute this latter claim although he does make use of the fact that such independent existence can be doubted, as will be explained. He does dispute, however, any claim that the realist might make that 'objects' so conceived constitute radical reality. Realism cannot provide the solidity and security required because it fails both of the tests referred to above: as a thesis it is neither autonomous nor universal. It cannot be universal because it leaves out of its account of reality a feature of the world which is implied in its very formulation.

Realism, says Ortega, 'affirms that what is real are things, but that is at the same time a thought of mine, and so while I think the exclusive reality of things, I am, in fact adding a different reality: that of the thought in which I think it' (OC 12, 112). In a slightly different formulation in *¿Qué es conocimiento?*, Ortega writes: 'When I have affirmed that "the world exists", and I look to see whether, in fact, everything which I can suspect might exist is implied in that affirmation, I immediately find that as well as the existence of the world, there is also the existence of my thinking in the world' (QC, 31). To the extent that the existence of thought is left out of realism's account of what there is in the world (and is indeed implied by its very formulation), realism cannot claim to be universal. For this reason, it cannot claim, either, to be a sustainable thesis in the context of the search for radical reality.

Realism's candidacy as a thesis on radical reality is further under-mined by the fact that, in Ortega's opinion, the objects on behalf of which it claims such status are not independent. I may be looking at a wall, for example, and would seem to be fully justified in asser-ting the independence of the wall from me. However, if I shut my eyes, I stop seeing it. Suddenly, I realise that I intervene in the fact of the wall 'being there'. In *Unas lecciones de metafísica* Ortega writes that, 'the thesis which affirms that Reality is the World, or is things, is complicated by another: that reality is a subject which thinks the world, or things' (OC 12, 106). In terms of being a candidate for the expression of radical reality, then, realism fails on two counts. First, the fact that its very formulation implies the existence of something other than objects (i.e. thought) means that it is not universal. For a reality to be radical it must be universal; therefore, realism cannot supply us with radical reality. Second, the objects which are realism's candidates for radical reality are not indepen-dent because their perception implies the existence of a perceiving subject. Thus realism also fails the test of autonomy. These two reasons combined disqualify realism as a sustainable thesis with respect to the nature of radical reality.

Idealism

According to Ortega, Descartes' genius was to recognise that the realist thesis was complicated by thought, and to turn this on its head by affirming that thought is what constitutes radical reality. Ortega asks, what remains when I doubt the existence of the world, of objects, of a wall? And he replies, paraphrasing Descartes himself, 'doubt – the fact that I doubt: if I doubt that the world exists, I can-not doubt that I doubt. Here we have the limit of all possible doubt' (OC 7, 365). As doubt is no more than a species of thought, Descartes is fully entitled, it seems, to say that what I cannot doubt is the fact of my thinking. To this extent, thought is an indubitable candidate for constituting the radical reality which Ortega is seek-ing. Furthermore, it appears that the idealist thesis complies with demands that it be universal and independent – in *¿Qué es conoci-miento?*, Ortega writes that: 'It seems that idealism's truth is ex-emplary in its self-sufficiency and its integrity. Because the only thing presupposed by the proposition "thought exists" is the act of thinking, the act in which it was thought. But it is clear that the thought with which I think that thought exists is already included in the thesis and does not add anything new' (QC, 32).

He concludes as follows: 'The reality of this wall is problematic, but the reality of my vision of the wall is indisputable. This, then, is the firm, dependable reality – that of my thoughts, of my ideas' (OC 12, 106). The delivery of just such a 'firm' reality is of course, in Ortega's opinion, what philosophy is supposed to accomplish. Philosophy is practised because life obliges some of us to make sense of it, and this 'making sense' involves the search for intellectual stability and orientation. Realism cannot provide such stability because it is complicated by thought – it is not sufficient unto itself. Idealism, however, appears to be complicated by nothing which is not already included in the thesis. Are we justified in concluding, then, that thought is the radical reality which life, through philosophy, demands that we find?

Criticisms of idealism

The first argument that Ortega deploys against idealism takes the following form. He notes that idealists generally speak of objects as the 'contents of consciousness', and asks whether this statement is not unintelligible – like talking of a round square (OC 7, 400). Continuing, in *¿Qué es filosofía?*, and referring to the theatre in which he was giving the course, he says that if the theatre does form a part of his consciousness then 'I am saying that something extended, with a height of twenty metres, coloured blue, etc., is genuinely a part of me'. But this would mean that 'my thought has a height of twenty metres and is so many metres wide – consequently, that I am extended, that my thought occupies space and that it is partly blue-coloured' (OC 7, 401). Confronted with this literal understanding of the phrase 'contents of consciousness', the idealist redeploys his argument and says: 'that which is a content of my thought or consciousness is, of course, only my thinking the theatre, the image of, or the imagining this theatre' (*ibid.*). The content of consciousness is now thought, and because thought is not extended and does not occupy space, it makes sense to say that the theatre as thought is a content of consciousness. The problem now for the idealist, however, is that the theatre has been left outside thought (*ibid.*). Precisely because it is the theatre as thought which is the content of consciousness, what I have in my mind, on this second reading, is my representation of the theatre rather than the theatre itself. In other words, the idealist has mended his or her position by changing the frame of reference, or 'moving the goalposts'.

Ortega takes this opportunity to draw a distinction between 'my representation' and 'what is being represented', or, more generally, 'my thinking' and 'what is being thought about'. They are not the same thing. Idealism, in sidestepping the first criticism directed at it, i.e. that it makes no sense to talk of my mind as being extended, slides over this distinction and begins talking of something different – my representation of an object rather than the object itself. Idealism, then, cannot talk sensibly of 'objects of consciousness', but only of 'representations of objects in consciousness'. In retreating to this second position, it leaves objects independently existing outside consciousness which, on the idealist reading, is not how or where they are supposed to be.

Ortega's second criticism turns on the notion that idealism presupposes a reality previous to thought, and thus fails the test of universality:

Now the surprising thing about this activity which we call 'thinking about something' derives from the fact that it can never be our primary or original involvement with that thing. That is to say that thinking about it can never be the first thing we do with it, but rather that in order to be able to indulge in this peculiar activity, it is clearly necessary that that something has been in a prior relation to me which is not merely thinking it or thinking about it.   (OC 12, 65)

Idealism, in other words, bases itself in the act of reflection. Ortega's response to this is that such an act can never constitute our primary relation to an object – rather it presupposes such a primary relation. The act of reflection is an act which objectifies the original involvement with the thing, i.e. which makes the original act an object for reflecting consciousness. In doing so, it never deals with the original act, but only with that act as an object for reflecting consciousness. As such, reflection is a form of 'second-order' reality – it is already an attitude towards reality, rather than reality in its radicality: 'The object of a conscious act is precisely that which is not the act, but where the act ends' (QC, 18). It would, of course, have been better for Ortega to have made more careful use of the word 'conscious' here. Generally speaking he makes no distinction between reflecting and non-reflecting consciousness (although this does not imply that he does not recognise that there is one). It is possible for us to be conscious without being reflectively conscious, and when Ortega uses the word 'conscious' or 'consciousness', he is invariably referring to reflective consciousness.

Now, if we want to put ourselves in touch with the act itself (that which, in Ortega's opinion, constitutes radical reality), then we have to go beyond or behind the reflective conscious act. Ortega contrasts the 'act itself' with the 'act of reflection' by naming them respectively executive (*ejecutivo*) and objective (*objetivo*). There is the executive act, which is primary, and the objective act, which makes the executive act an object for consciousness, and which is secondary:

It is necessary, then, to distinguish between the executive being of thought or consciousness and its objective being. Thought, in terms of execution, or as something carrying itself out (*ejecutándose*) (and while it is carrying itself out it is not an object for itself), does not exist for itself. Therefore it does not make sense to call it thought. In order for there to be a thought, it is necessary that it has already carried itself out and that I contemplate it, or make it an object for me, from outside . . . when there is only thought there is not genuinely that which was thought in it. When there is only my seeing that wall, there is no wall. Thought, therefore, is a conviction no longer in force (*vigente*) – it is no longer carrying itself out, but rather looks at the conviction from outside . . . the only conviction in force is the present (*actual*) one, the acting (*actuante*) one, the one which does not yet exist for me and which, therefore, is not thought but absolute position.

(OC 12, 118)

From this perspective, idealism's error lies in ascribing primacy to the conscious act, whereas what is in fact primary is the pre-intellectual relationship I have with objects. Ortega, in *Unas lecciones de metafísica*, sums this up as follows:

In my opinion, this is the decisive point: when idealism refers to what is immediate as thought, it contradicts and does damage to its own invulnerable starting-point. This consisted in demanding immediacy as the fundamental and unavoidable character of reality – its presence and evidence before me. But the thing is that when I see that wall, it is the wall which is present and evident, and not my seeing it. I do not see my seeing when I am seeing. In order to realise that there is such a thing as my seeing, I have to stop seeing and remember that a moment ago I was seeing. I see my seeing when I am outside it, when it is not immediate to me, when the reality with which it had to do – seeing the wall – is reality no longer, but rather I am in another reality which I call 'remembering a past [event]': remembering that I saw the wall.   (OC 12, 124)

The executive act, then, is the fundamental act, and anything which comes after it and reflects on it can be no more than a theory on, and interpretation of, the original act. Doing comes before reflecting, thinking presupposes execution, and so idealism is not sustainable as a thesis on what constitutes radical reality:

we have just seen . . . that seeing is not congruent with the act of seeing; that a thought does not and cannot think itself. In a word, this means that that reality – consciousness, cogitatio, or thought – far from being such reality [i.e. radical reality] is no more than an invention, a hypothesis, a theory. Therefore it cannot be of use in terms of being fundamental reality, as absolutely real reality, because it comprises a pseudo-principle.

(OC 12, 179)

This conclusion has repercussions for Ortega's theory of knowledge. According to him, what we think is never reality, but only a reflection on it. Radical reality is that which there is previous to, and presupposed by, any interpretation of it, and this is the only reality which can satisfy our living need for intellectual stability. This pre-theoretical reality will be that which exists before it is looked at or made an object. The world is not our interpretation of it – rather that interpretation presupposes the reality of the world as it is previous to interpretation. If the world is always something other than what we think about it, then how are we ever to get to know it? Ortega writes: 'The act of knowing . . . is a return journey. First – take note – we have to form ideas of things for ourselves, and this is what has always been done up to now. But then, so as to truly know, it is necessary to subtract all of that which has been thought, realising that reality is always different, more or less, from that which is thought' (OC 12, 234). The precise nature of this subtraction will become clear in chapter 10. Now we only need note that the radical reality which Ortega seeks is the presupposition of the theories we have about it. In this context, Ortega notes that Descartes made a mistake in supposing that doubt was equivalent to thought. Doubt, says Ortega, is a species of thought. If I was not a theorising being, I would not doubt. My existence as a doubting being, then, is part of a wider existence as a theorising being. But in turn, I theorise for something – I theorise because I need to, because my life and the problems it poses demand that I theorise. My theorising, then, and my doubting, presuppose my life.

Ortega's expression of the error in Descartes' reasoning is to be found in *En el centenario de una universidad* (On the centenary of a university), a speech given in Granada in 1935:

Without doubt, you have come to a conclusion by thinking: I exist because I think. But remember that you set about thinking at a certain point in time, that you caught on to the fact of your thinking not 'just like that', but because beforehand you felt lost in a strange, problematic, unsafe and doubtful environment, whose character appeared odd to you. You set about thinking, then, 'because' you existed beforehand, and that your existence consisted in finding yourself shipwrecked in something which is called the world, which one does not know anything about, which is doubtful (and therefore which is different from you because, as you assure us, one cannot doubt [the existence of] oneself). To live, or to exist, is not to be alone but rather, on the contrary, it is to be not able to be alone with oneself: to be fenced in and unsure, as a prisoner of some other mysterious, heterogeneous thing – circumstance, the Universe. And so as to find some security in it, you set about thinking, in the same way in which a shipwrecked sailor moves his arms about and swims. I do not exist because I think, but vice versa: I think because I exist. Thought is not the unique and primary reality but vice versa: thought or intelligence comprise one of the reactions which life obliges us to make. It has its roots and its meaning in the radical, prior and terrible fact of living. Pure and isolated reason has to learn to be 'reason from life's point of view' (razón vital).

(OC 4, 472)

If Descartes had realised that his doubting implied his living, then he would not have made reflective consciousness the radical datum, or as the only fact of which he could have certain knowledge. Indeed, for any theoretical proposition to exist, there must also exist a pre-intellectual reality which gives rise to it. What, then, is this radical reality which gives rise to all others, and in which all others are founded?

Radical reality

Neither objects nor reflective consciousness can satisfy the demands of autonomy and universality made by what would constitute radical reality. Objects presuppose thought and a thinking subject, while thought, or reflection, presupposes an executive act prior to reflection. Realism and idealism, in other words, are both complicated by a reality previous to them, and this is the reality which Ortega hopes to demonstrate to be the radical reality with which life, through philosophy, demands that we make contact.

From Ortega's criticism of idealism, it will be remembered that the theatre of which he spoke could neither intelligibly be said to be inside consciousness, nor outside it, in the sense of independent from it. He asks, 'Where, then, in a word, is the theatre? The answer is obvious: it is not inside my thought as a part of it, but neither is it outside my thought if by 'outside' we mean that it has nothing to do with it. It is together with, inseparably together with, my thinking it – neither inside nor outside, but with my thought, as the obverse goes with the reverse and the left with the right, without the left being the right or the obverse being the reverse' (OC 7, 401). The executive act, which is more radical than any act of reflection, is constituted by my coexistence with things. This coexistence is the radical datum from which all others are derived, says Ortega. It is reality previous to any interpretation of it, and presupposed by any such interpretation. When I see a wall, then, what there is is myself and the wall, absolutely and irreducibly inseparable. When I see my seeing the wall, on the other hand, I have made my 'seeing-the-wall' an object for consciousness, and the original executive act has passed into the past. In seeing my seeing-the-wall I am still, of course, coexisting with things, but the particular executive act is now different.

In a long footnote in *La idea del principio en Leibniz*, Ortega sums up this position via a consideration of Husserl's phenomenological method, of which Ortega had made a remarkably rapid assimilation as early as 1913, the same year as the publication of Husserl's *Ideen zu einer reinen Phänomenologie*. The following lengthy quotation has the merit of first, summarising Ortega's opinion of the phenomenological method, as expressed in Husserl; second, formally proposing the coexistence of myself with things as the basic reality; and third, giving a name to this coexistence – human life. From this derives the central feature, the nodal point, of Ortega's philosophy – individual human life as the radical reality.

Ever since 1914 (see my *Meditaciones del Quijote* in *Obras Completas*, volume 1), the intuition of the phenomenon of 'human life' has been the basis of my whole thought. At that time I formulated it in the context of several courses I gave on the Phenomenology of Husserl, radically correcting the description of the phenomenon 'consciousness of . . .' which, as is well-known, constitutes, in turn, the basis of his doctrine. . . Reduced to its barest bones, my opening objection to Phenomenology is the following: Husserl recognises that consciousness is constitutively positioning and he calls this the 'natural attitude of consciousness'. Phenomenology consists in describing this phenomenon of natural consciousness from the standpoint of a reflective consciousness which contemplates the former without 'taking it seriously', without accompanying it in its positions, i.e. by suspending its 'executivity', or its executive quality. I oppose this from two (*sic*) points of view. First, the suspension of that which I call the executive character of consciousness, its positioning character, is to deprive it of that which is most constitutive of it, and thus of consciousness as a whole. Second, we thus suspend the executive quality of one consciousness from the standpoint of another, the reflective – which Husserl calls the 'phenomenological reduction' – without the latter having any determinate superiority in terms of nullifying the primary and reflected consciousness. Third, it [Husserl's phenomenology] allows, on the other hand, the execution of the reflective consciousness, and it allows this consciousness to give the character of absolute being to the primary consciousness, calling it *Erlebnis* or lived experience (*vivencia*). This shows precisely that all consciousness has executive validity, and it does not make sense to have one consciousness nullify another. We can reasonably nullify any of our given acts of consciousness, as we do when we put right a mistake like, for example, an optical illusion; but if we set an 'illusory' consciousness against a 'normal' consciousness without any mediating set of reasons, the latter cannot nullify the former. Perception and hallucination have, in themselves, equal rights.

A consequence of these objections is that since 1914 I have set forth a description of the phenomenon 'consciousness of', revealing that – in opposition to the whole of idealism – to say that the act of consciousness is real but its object is only intentional and therefore unreal is not pure description, but is already a hypothesis. I said then that the description which is rigorously congruent with the phenomenon, is that which says that in a phenomenon of consciousness such as perception, we find the coexistence of the I and the thing, i.e. that this is not ideality or intentionality, but reality itself. In this way, what there is in the 'fact' of perception is the following: myself, on the one hand, being towards the perceived object, and, on the other hand, the perceived object towards me – or, what amounts to the same thing – that there is no such phenomenon as 'consciousness of', in terms of a general state of mind. What there is is the reality which is myself opening itself up and enduring the reality of my surroundings which acts on me, and the supposed description of the phenomenon 'consciousness' resolves itself into a description of the phenomenon 'real human life', as the coexistence of the I with the things around it which constitute its circumstance. It turns out, then, that 'there is' no consciousness in terms of phenomenon, but rather that consciousness is a hypothesis – precisely the hypothesis which we have inherited from Descartes. This is the reason why Husserl reverts to Descartes.

(OC 8, 272–5 fn)

Ortega's analysis of idealism and of phenomenology (which he characterises elsewhere as the most sophisticated form of idealism) thus leads him to the conclusion that radical reality is constituted by my coexistence with things. Realism held that the world was independent of thought, and idealism held that thought was independent of the world. Ortega argues that neither independent world nor independent thought 'exist' – that these theses are mere constructions or inventions, rather than reality. What there is, radically, is the coexistence of myself with things, a pre-theoretical reality from which all others derive and on which they depend.

Further, Ortega asks: what name can we give to this radical reality? 'Now, that absolute reality in which an I has to count on that which [it] is not, and by token of which its existence is irremediably an existing in the other, outside of itself: what is it if not living?' (OC 12, 127). Ortega would claim that by making a disinterested analysis of two other theses about what constitutes primary reality, he has 'stumbled across' human life as the radical reality which is presupposed by all others. He would say he did not set out to prove that this is so. He merely set out to ask whether realism and idealism were suppositionless theses about radical reality. He discovered that realism's candidate for radical reality, the independent object, presupposes thought and a thinking subject, and thus is neither autonomous nor universal. He discovered that idealism's candidate, independent thought, presupposes a reason for that thought and a context in which it takes place, as well as presupposing a pre-intellectual executive act. Neither candidate, then, can provide the firmness and solidity required by the conditions which radical reality has to fulfill.

It turns out, at the same time, that the pre-intellectual executive act consists in the coexistence of myself with things. Further, this coexistence of myself with things is what we normally call 'life', and it is this which Ortega feels entitles him to refer to individual human life as the radical reality.

Human life as radical reality

Ortega's *yo soy yo y mi circunstancia* (I am I and my circumstance) from the *Meditaciones del Quijote* of 1914 comprises an early intuition of the idea that a comprehensive description of the subject will not be obtained as long as it is conceived of as separate from its object. Recast in terms derived from his later work, we might say that 'I' and 'circumstance' are both abstractions of, or theories about, that radical reality which Ortega denominates 'human life'. Beyond the claims of idealism and realism he discovers a fundamental relationship between subject and object, a never-ending to-ing and fro-ing between me and the world: a relationship *within which* consciousness and objects become apparent and on which they depend. It 'just so happens' that this relationship, this endless 'dealing with' (*tratar con*) the world, is precisely that which we habitually call 'life'. In this way, a common, everyday word becomes elevated to the status of a technical, philosophical term. The 'accidental' nature of this ought to be stressed, so as to rescue the sense that Ortega conveys of a disinterested enquiry into radical reality.

This is how he puts it in *¿Qué es filosofía?*: 'It is not my existence, or myself existing, which is the radical datum, or the datum which can be complicated no further, but rather my coexistence with the world' (OC 7, 403). Then he asks:

> But what have we here? What have we accidentally come across? Just this: that basic fact of someone who sees, loves and hates the world, and who moves in it, struggles in it and suffers on its account – this is what from time immemorial, and in the most humble and universal vocabulary, has been called 'my life'. What is this? Simply that fundamental reality, the fact of all facts, the datum for the universe, that which is given to me is . . . 'my life' – not only my I (*mi yo*), not my hermetic consciousness, because these are already interpretations: the idealist interpretation.
>
> (*ibid.*).

It will not have escaped notice that Ortega here makes yet more concrete his notion of what constitutes radical reality. It is not human life in general, but *my* life, that of each and every person (*la vida de cada cual*) as it is experienced individually. I cannot consider human life in general, or even that of my neighbour, as the radical reality, because I soon see that my neighbour's life appears in mine – in other words, that my life is a precondition of theirs appearing to me. To the extent that their life presupposes mine, as far as I am concerned it is my life which is radical, and theirs which is derivative. Their life, therefore, cannot constitute radical reality, although I realise that my neighbour's life, although derivative (for me), is itself another concrete radical reality, albeit someone else's.

Radical reality, then, remains defined as my life and this, according to Antonio Rodríguez Huéscar, is Ortega's most important metaphysical innovation: 'his discovery or intuition of the irreducible, of the radical reality of life, as that which is truly immediate and impossible to doubt'. It is radical because it satisfies Ortega's demand that such a reality should be self-sufficient. If one could find something that was demonstrably outside of, or presupposed by human life, then life could not be a *radical* reality. But, according to Ortega, it happens that everything is found in, or is rooted in (*radica en*), my life. My life presupposes the existence of nothing else; on the contrary, everything else is presupposed by my life. Even a transcendent God, generally supposed to exist beyond the world, would be found in my life. The existence of a transcendent God presupposes my life, argues Ortega, in that He appears within it and could never appear outside it.

A worthwhile critique of Ortega's principle of *individual* human life as radical reality would require more space than is available here, but two possible lines of objection may be pointed out. The first is simply that the awareness of self could be argued to presuppose the awareness of other selves. If I need other selves to be aware of my self, then which is the more 'radical' datum? In other words, one can follow Ortega to the point of saying that I become aware of other lives through my own individual life, but it may be objected that my individuation would not be possible without other 'individuations' against which to check my own. At the same time, the awareness of myself as an individual is a self-conscious awareness which therefore, on Ortega's own terms, ought not to be an awareness of radical reality. It could be argued that our pre-intellectual – and therefore radical – experience is one of un-individuated collectivism, and that individuation is a product of conscious reflection. If this is so, it renders problematic Ortega's denomination of individual human life as radical reality.

Be that as it may, the presuppositionless nature of human life is expressed by Ortega in *¿Qué es conocimiento?* as follows:

the fact of my life, with which and within which I find myself, appears not to be conditioned by any other. My life does not exist conditionally – it exists absolutely: up to the point where every other fact or reality – and note this well – already presupposes the fact of my life in which they appear to me and in which I receive notification of them. And let it not be said as an objection to the independence of my life's reality, that it has a cause, because that – the recognition that it has a cause, the search for it and, perhaps, the finding of it – are the workings of my life, and they imply the existence, *impliciter*, of it. Note, then, that the fact or reality of my life is previous to, and presupposed by, every other fact. (QC, 109)

Similar expressions can be found throughout Ortega's mature work (OC 7, 405; 7, 424; 12, 193; QC, 52 and QC, 109 for example). My life is not fundamental in that it is the smallest element one can find, or in the sense in which the physicist's so-called 'ultimate particle' would constitute the universe's basic building-block. It is fundamental in that it is that reality where all others meet and through which they flow. There are things – from the shortest-lived sub-atomic particle to the oldest of the earth's rocks – and there is consciousness; but both, in Ortega's opinion, are abstractions in terms of the search for radical reality. My life is fundamental in that everything is rooted in it.

The problem of knowing my life

Behind Ortega's conception of what human life is lurks a problem of knowledge. If, when I objectify something, I am not seeing the something, then how can I 'get inside' the to-ing and fro-ing which is my life? If I want to see my life 'in action', then is it possible to do so without turning that action into an object and thus losing the quality of that which constituted the original action?

The answer would appear to be, no. The immediate presence which is life, or the executive act, can never be experienced in its immediacy because 'experiencing' necessarily involves reflection. Reflection, on Ortega's reading, involves objectification and, once objectified, the executive act is executive no longer, but only a reflection on it. Ortega expresses the situation metaphorically as follows: 'Note that of all the points on the earth, the only one which we cannot observe directly is that which is under our feet' (OC 7, 413). Thus, an unavoidable consequence of our standing in a particular spot is that that spot will never be directly visible to us (so long as we stay standing on it, and do not jump, of course). So it is with the executive act. While we are 'doing' it, it is not possible to perceive it because each perception is itself a new executive act. No executive act is recoverable in its immediacy and purity.

The fact that Ortega's radical reality can never itself be an object for knowledge does not mean, of course, that nothing can be said of it. Although the actual act cannot be intellectualised, Ortega evidently believes that the generic character of such acts can be glimpsed and described. Our standing on a spot precludes us from seeing that spot, but the fact of our standing presupposes the existence of something beneath our feet. We deduce what there must be beneath our feet to make the fact of our standing possible. Ortega's metaphysical argument about human life as radical reality takes a similar form. He asks whether idealism or realism themselves make any presuppositions, and discovers that they both presuppose that executive act, or that immediate co-presence of myself and an object, which he calls human life.

He claims that I am aware of myself as living (in the immediate sense which he gives the word) in a pre-intellectual, pre-theoretical fashion:

Now, that which I call 'I' is constantly and infallibly present to me – so much so that it constitutes me and totally includes my very existence. I am present to myself without it being necessary to perceive myself . . . That reality 'life' is a field of reflection in itself where everything is absolutely 'being-towards-itself'. I am not the place in which this reflection happens – rather I find myself immersed in the reflection, like being bathed in a light. Life illuminates itself and everything in it has a quality of self-illumination and self-phosphorescence.   (QC, 20)

My life, proposes Ortega, could not exist simply as an object for me, for then it would be intermittent in the sense that it would only 'exist' when I had made it an object of perception. The idea of my life being intermittent is problematic and so Ortega presupposes a continually existing human life which is always 'pre-cognitively' (QC, 54) present to me.

The example he habitually gives to illustrate the quality of this immediate, pre-intellectual presence is that of toothache. The pain which a bad tooth gives me is not 'thought' by me, but rather is an immediate pain which I feel without the relationship between me and the pain being brought to the level of intellectual awareness: 'Toothache exists or is towards me without there being any distance in between . . . the "being towards me" here does not mean that it is an object for me, an object which I perceive, think, imagine, etc., but rather that the pain's relation to me is direct, and consists not in being an object for me, but rather immediately and absolutely in "hurting-me"' (QC, 54). Ortega applies exactly the same principle to my relationship with objects. The radical reality of an object's relation to me is not my thinking or perceiving it, but rather lies in its immediately 'being-towards-me'. We shall look at this more closely in chapter 10.

It might still be objected, in any case, that Ortega's description of that pre-intellectual relationship between myself and my toothache has been arrived at by a process which is itself intellectual and thus theoretical rather than immediate. And if, as Ortega holds, reality is more or less never that which is thought about it, why should we pay any more attention to his description of our relationship with our toothache than to anyone else's?

In the first place, he claims that he is not 'forming a theory *about*

our life, but rather describing it in the same way as I might describe
that wall' (OC 12, 46). He is well aware of the criticism that might
be levelled at him: 'We have to undo the objective conception of the
'world' which credulous thought has given us and carry it back to
a conception of the 'world' or of reality, as execution, or carrying
itself out (*ejecutividad*). In the sense of it being a conception, ours too
will be objectification, or thought which we carry out. But the difference between this and the normal credulous use of thought is that
we are going to make it look at reality from its own point of view'
(QC, 51). His technique, as expressed here, involves accepting that
objectification will take place, and then subtracting it from the
perception so as to get at 'pre-objectified' reality. This reality is
glimpsed or inferred by considering what is presupposed by objectified reality. That presupposition will be naked, or radical, reality.

To this extent, says Ortega, his method is entirely opposed to that
of Husserl's phenomenology, which seeks to make an inspection of
consciousness by 'bracketing-off' the external causes and effects of
the conscious or intellectual process. He says: 'Our subject of enquiry, then, is strictly the reverse of phenomenology and, therefore,
of its method. When phenomenology describes an act it eliminates
or *limits* its executive character. We are *exclusively* concerned with
this executive character. We do not take the act as it appears as an
object for reflection, but rather we suspend this unavoidable reflection' (*ibid.*). Ortega's intention is to wallow in the executive act –
for he believes that this, far from being a distortion of reality, is
actually what constitutes it. Elsewhere he describes his method as an
'un-' or 'de-thinking' all that is already thought – perhaps best conceived of as an 'unknowing'. Although this 'de-thinking' will also be
a thinking, he claims that it will be neither gullible nor credulous:

Of course it is true that in describing life we have set about thinking about
it. But in this unique case, what our thought is looking for and what it proposes to do is precisely to discover living reality in all its nakedness – that
which it is when it is nothing but what it is, when everything we have
thought *about* it or because of it and which it is not, is removed *from* it. In
a word, in this *unique* case our thought struggles to un-think (*despensar*) all
those thoughts which we think in our life.   (OC 12, 62–3)

My relation to my executive act, then, is one of immediate
presence. My relationship with my life, which is constituted by an
enormous quantity of executive acts, is described in the same way.
The quality of the executive act itself, and therefore of my life,

can never be captured intellectually because such cognition implies a new executive act which turns the original one into an object of perception. I can never be aware of my life *as* absolute, immediate presence, but I can be aware of my life as *consisting in* absolute, immediate presence. Thus I constantly 'count on' (*contar con*) my life and everything in it. Naked reality will only be that from which all previous thought has been removed, and although Ortega recognises that that removal will itself be an intellectual act, it will not be gullible, innocent or credulous, for it will be aimed at revealing what reality really is and it will know what to do in order to arrive at a description of such reality. The method which Ortega proposes will be discussed in the final chapter.

Conclusion

With individual human life established as the radical reality, philosophy has accomplished the task posed by life itself. We philosophise because life demands that we seek intellectual security. Philosophy is one of the activities in which some human beings have engaged to satisfy this need. Such security will only be found if a principle can be expressed which is autonomous and universal. Ortega's opinion is that human life, as radical reality, comprises just such a principle. We can see now more clearly why he concluded that philosophy is founded in, and presupposes, human life. If everything has its root in human life and is to be found in it (including God), then philosophy, too, must be founded in it. Philosophy is one of the many things we do in our lives, as a result of being alive: 'We philosophise because we live' (OC 12, 191), he concludes.

9

Perspectivism and truth

In his *A Dictionary of Philosophy*, Professor Antony Flew (or one of his contributors) has written the following on 'perspectivism': 'The view that the external world is to be interpreted through different alternative systems of concepts and beliefs and that there is no authoritative independent criterion for determining that one such system is more valid than another. Perspectivism occurs in many of the writings of Nietzsche, but is best known from the work of Ortega y Gasset' (1984: 226). It is important that such mistaken impressions be rectified, and it is one of the aims of this chapter to do just that. To imply that Ortega does not believe that there can be an 'authoritative independent criterion' for deciding between different perspectives is at best misleading, and at worst, wrong. However, although perspectivism is one of the best-known features of Ortega's thought, it by no means exhausts his ideas about truth. Generally speaking, his reflections on perspectivism are confined to the period prior to that with which this section on his philosophy has primarily been concerned. More specifically, it is in his 1923 book *El tema de nuestro tiempo*, that the notion receives its most sustained treatment. I propose to deal with it in this chapter precisely because it is an idea with which most people will associate Ortega, but I also propose to examine the reflections on truth found in his mature thought. This will illustrate that perspectivism, although central to his thought and never rejected by him, is by no means his last word on the subject of truth.

Perspectivism

In Section X of *El tema de nuestro tiempo* entitled 'The doctrine of the point of view', Ortega says that from different positions two people see the same surroundings. However, they do not see the same thing. Their different positions mean that the surroundings are

organised in a different way: what is in the foreground for one may
be in the background for another. Furthermore, as things are hidden
one behind another, each person will see some thing which the other
may not.

Ortega then asks whether it would make sense for one person to
say that the other's view of their surroundings was false. Evidently
not, he replies. But neither would it make sense for them to agree
to differ and then to say that their views of the surroundings were
illusory, for that would assume the existence of a third, authentic,
set of surroundings not subject to the same conditions as theirs.
Ortega emphasises that this archetypal set of surroundings does not
and cannot exist, and that the idea of a reality which would look the
same from any point of view is absurd. His conclusion is that,
'Cosmic reality is such that it can only be seen from a given perspective. *Perspective is one of the components of reality*. Far from being its
deformation, it is its organisation' (OC 3, 199). This, in essence, is
Ortega's doctrine of perspectivism.

At this stage it is important to stress that Ortega is not simply
referring us to the phenomenon of visual perspective. It is true that
nobody sees the same thing as anybody else because we are all in different locations, but at the same time we bring to bear a different
way of seeing things. This manner of seeing things will depend upon
a whole range of necessities, appetites, desires, feelings and intellectual preoccupations – in sum, all those elements which comprise
me as an individual. The distance from objects is not, then, merely
spatial, but affective as well.

Ortega provides a vivid example of this phenomenon in a section
of his essay 'Vitalidad, alma, espíritu' (Vitality, soul, spirit) (1924)
which he calls 'Sentimental geometry'. The title is revelatory in that
the thrust of his argument is to show that the structure of the world
we perceive is affected by the feelings we have for it. He talks of a
friend's reaction to the absence from Madrid of his beloved,
Soledad. In a sense Madrid stays the same – the same trees, parks
and squares, the same noise of trams and motorhorns, the same
streets and houses. But Ortega's friend's perception of all this has
changed in that a dimension of its reality is missing. When Soledad
was in Madrid it had a centre: her house, and a periphery: that
which surrounded her house. What was near and what was far was
determined by the presence of Soledad in the city. 'Now I see', says
Ortega's friend, 'to what extent my love for Soledad spread through

the city and stimulated my life in it. Now I notice that the most remote things, things which seemed to have least to do with Soledad, had acquired an additional quality through being related to her, and that for me that quality was the most important' (OC 2, 463). Furthermore, the place where Soledad has gone to stay used to have no significance whatever, but now it takes on a dimension of reality which it never had before.

Ortega's perspectivism, then, is not confined to the visual field, but has to take account of the affective relationship between subject and object. This is the more profound meaning of his assertion that subject and object should not be defined in terms of mutual contradiction, but rather as mutually complementary. Subject informs object and object informs subject – either one without the other is an abstraction.

Ortega's position up to this point seems clear and beyond reproach. In fact it responds to a whole host of reactions which we all encounter every day of our lives. We have all experienced, for example, the phenomenon of distance changing in accordance with state of mind – the breathless anticipation of meeting a loved one can turn the shortest train journey into a trans-continental trek. Time, too, is affected by sentiment – the twelve hours of the night of Christmas Eve for a young child are an eternity compared to the twelve hours which elapse before a visit to the dentist. This dilation and contraction of time and distance is a fact of human life which Ortega attempts to make a part of his philosophy. The interaction between subject and object leads him to what he calls perspectivism, a doctrine which holds that perception is irremediably subjective and that any philosophy which refuses to take that fact into account is bound to begin from false premises. Ortega's belief that perspective is one of the components of reality clearly preserves the subjective nature of perception and responds to facts of our everyday experience.

But at what cost? In the example of the two people looking at the same countryside and seeing two different things, Ortega made it clear that the notion of a third 'authentic' countryside was absurd. Again, beyond the sentimental reaction of Ortega's friend to the absence of his lover, is there a real, objective, Madrid? Or are we reduced to saying that Madrid is what anyone cares to say it is? Again, in what sense, if any, are the twelve hours of the child on Christmas Eve the same as the twelve hours I endure waiting to go to the dentist? Irrevocably, Ortega's doctrine of perspectivism leads us to inquire as to his vision of truth.

Against relativism and rationalism

In the first instance, it is useful to summarise the two notions of truth which Ortega is attempting to supersede and which he calls rationalism and relativism. The problem resides in the fact that on the one hand we want truth to be unique and invariable so that it adequately reflects 'what things are' (OC 3, 157). But on the other hand, history shows that we have constantly changed our opinion as to what the truth is. How, then, are we to square the truth, which must be invariable, with our changing interpretations of it?

The relativists' response is to drop one side of the equation by affirming that there is no such thing as invariable truth. They say that we each have our own convictions which for us are the truth. 'The' truth, then, does not exist; there are only truths 'relative' to each subject. Ortega is happy with this position only to the extent that it seeks to preserve the concrete changeability which characterises human life and experience, and that it attempts to be impartial in the face of a welter of historical facts and phenomena. But then, he asks: if truth does not exist, how can relativism take itself seriously? And second, 'faith in the truth is a radical fact of human life' (OC 3, 158). If we amputate the truth, then human life is rendered absurd – indeed, the amputation itself would make no sense. Relativism, he says, winds up as scepticism, and scepticism is suicide. Third, circumstantial evidence against relativism is provided by the possibility of understanding other peoples and other periods of history:

The minimum presupposition of history is that the subject of whom we speak can be understood. Now, one cannot understand something which does not represent even a partial truth. A complete error would not register with us because we would not understand it. The profound presupposition of history, then, is completely opposed to radical relativism. When one begins to study primitive man, one supposes that their culture had meaning and truth and that if it had both these things, then it still has them. (OC 7, 285)

The physiological implication of the word 'amputate', above, is no accident in Ortega. We know now that thinking, for him, is as much of a necessity as breathing. Further, he says that thinking –

if it is to have any sense at all – must involve thinking about the truth. 'Its mission', he goes on, 'is to reflect the world of things and to accommodate itself to them in one way or another. In sum, to think is to think the truth' (OC 3, 164). With hindsight one can see how this is tightened up in his later work with his idea of life being constituted by a sense of being lost, and our consequent search for intellectual security through activities such as philosophy. As long as one does not have the truth one remains insecure. Truth, then, becomes a necessity which life demands of us in that if we do not think truthfully we shall never be satisfied with our conclusions, and to be dissatisfied with our conclusions is to remain insecure. In sum, relativism's *logical* fallacy lies in its constituting its own undermining, while its *intuitive* fallacy is that it does not respond adequately to that necessity for the truth without which human life would be rendered meaningless.

Rationalism, on the other hand, commits a different set of errors: 'in order to hang on to the truth it renounces life' (OC 3, 158), says Ortega. Rationalists believe that the truth is unique, absolute and invariable and consequently cannot be attributed to changeable human beings. Beyond the concrete, individual human being, they say, there must be something common to every Chinese, German and American – a kind of abstract subject. The problem with this, he continues, is that human life has disappeared: 'Note the way in which the self has been split up. On the one hand lies all that we concretely and vitally are – our palpitating and historical reality. On the other lies that nucleus of rationality which allows us to reach the truth but which, in exchange, does not live. It is a ghostly unreality which changelessly slips across time, alien to the fluctuations which are a symptom of life' (*ibid.*). On this reading, the world of truth is the quantitative world, the world of geometry. The qualitative, immediate world, the world we touch, see and hear, is relegated to secondary status.

He sums up his opposition to the dichotomy of rationalism and relativism in the following way: 'Rationalism keeps a hold on truth and abandons life. Relativism prefers the mobility of existence to the tranquil changelessness of truth' (OC 3, 163) – and the problem remains: 'How to reconcile one with the other?' (OC 3, 157). Ortega believes that perspectivism provides the solution to this problem and one has to have recourse to this at every turn in order to see how he attempts to avoid falling into either rationalist or relativist positions.

Two metaphors

It has been established that for the rationalist there exists a kind of abstract subject to which abstract knowledge is available. Ortega rejects this on the grounds that it does not take into account the variability and historicity of concrete human life. The assumption of the rationalist which Ortega challenges is that the point of view of the individual is false – a distortion of reality. Ortega has a favourite metaphor to describe his version of the relationship between me as subject and the reality which surrounds me – that of a sieve in a current of water. The sieve, depending on its characteristics, allows some things to pass and catches others. One would say that the sieve *selects*, but does not *deform*. 'This', says Ortega, 'is the subject's function, the function of the living being faced with the cosmic reality which surrounds it' (OC 3, 198).

A feature of the subject, as illustrated by this metaphor, is that he or she is a passive receptor of surrounding reality. We remember, though, that Ortega charcterises human life as a to-ing and fro-ing between subject and object. The two are not to be defined in mutual opposition, he says, but rather the subject is a 'going out' to the world around. This active aspect is caught in a second metaphor presented in an article on Einstein which further aims to emphasise that perspective is a component of reality, not its deformation. Ortega writes that when we see a billiard ball on a table, the only qualities we perceive are those of colour and shape. However, when that ball is struck by another one, another quality of the ball is revealed – its springiness. Further, this new quality is only revealed when it enters into contact with another object. Ortega continues: 'Now when one reality comes into contact with that other object which we call the "conscious subject", reality responds by *appearing* to it. The appearance is an objective quality of the real, and constitutes its reply to a subject' (OC 3, 236). Crucially for his argument that perspective is a component of reality and not its deformation, he goes on to say that the 'reply' of the object will be different according to the condition of the 'conscious subject' with which it comes into contact. The full importance of this will be pointed out shortly.

We might agree, then, that with these metaphors Ortega has effectively circumvented the rationalist position of the belief in the abstract subject to which knowledge, undeformed, is accessible. We

have a picture of a concrete subject which acts as a selector of surrounding reality, and the selections made are a constituent part of
that reality. Ortega has preserved the concrete variability of human
life which, precisely, was his aim when he set out to combat the
claims and implications of the rationalist version of truth. But,
again, at what cost? Has he not retreated into the relativist camp by
saying that every subject has access to a certain portion of the truth?
No two sieves are identical, to be sure, but every thing that every
sieve catches will be a portion of reality. On this reading every subject's vision or opinion will be true.

However it is important to stress two differences between Ortega
and the relativist. In the first place the relativist not only holds that
one's view is dependent upon one's position – a fact with which
Ortega would agree – but also that there is no way of deciding
whether one person's view is more 'true' than another's. Ortega
would most certainly not share this contention, and we shall see his
reasons in a moment.

A further factor is that although we might agree that Ortega's
is a relative conception of truth in that my view depends upon who
and where I am, it is also an absolute conception of truth in that
his doctrine of perspectivism makes reality itself relative. Better
still, his denial of the existence of an absolute reality above, beyond,
and separate from human life means that he also rejects the idea
of a truth relative to that absolute reality. As Paulino Garagorri
expresses it: 'Whoever denies the existence of an absolute truth
will be anything but a relativist with respect to that truth' (1970:
95). In other words, relativism is the flip-side of the absolutist
coin. If we abandon absolutism, relativism makes no sense. In
his account of individual human life as *the* radical reality, Ortega
has abandoned absolutism, so to charge him with relativism is
disingenuous. We remember, further, that perspective is a component of reality, not its deformation. Reality *can only* be appre-
hended perspectivally. Ortega gives us his clearest expression of
the relativity of reality in an article on Einstein, whose theory
he considers to be a marvellous confirmation of his own notion of
perspectivism.

He notes that for Newton and Galileo all our measurements of
movement, space and time were seen as relative to one another in
that they were measured against an 'out there' consisting of an
absolute movement, space and time. To this extent there are two

realities – one, absolute and inaccessible; and a second, relative and a mere approximation to the absolute.

However, if we abandon the notion of absolute space and time, then any measurements we make will necessarily be the only ones which express reality. This reality which the observer perceives will be a relative reality, but since this relative reality is now the only one there is (free of any comparison with 'absolute' reality), then it is also in principle the true, or absolute, reality. In conclusion, Ortega says: 'As far as the old relativism is concerned, our knowledge is relative because *that which* we aspire to know (tempo-spatial reality) is absolute and we never get there. But for Einstein's physics our knowledge is absolute: what is relative is reality' (OC 3, 233).

We stress, then, that Ortega would consider himself a relativist to the extent that my point of view is relative to who and where I am. But to the extent that reality itself is relative, then my relative position is at the same time an absolute position. If I conceive of myself as a sieve in a current of water, then what I catch will be dependent upon the configuration of my lattice and where I am in the current; but everything I catch will, necessarily, be something from that current of water. One might want to argue that there is an 'absolute' current of water 'out there', but it is an abstraction to talk about an 'out there' without talking about a person for whom it is 'out there'. What is concrete is the sieve in the water catching some of the innumerable particles which go to make up the current.

We have still to look at Ortega's refusal to agree with the relativist that all truths are of equal status, but it is worth taking a moment to flesh out an implication of his thesis of a 'relative reality' of which each one of us has absolute knowledge. We know that our individual 'peculiarities', far from being an obstacle to our obtaining of truth, allow us to receive a portion of the truth which may not be accessible to anyone else. Every individual, or group of individuals, comprises an 'irreplaceable observatory' on reality, holds Ortega, and he is faithful to this conception in some apparently unlikely places – in *La rebelión de las masas*, for example. Discussing bolshevism and fascism, he writes of, 'the positive aspects of their respective doctrines which, taken separately, evidently represent partial truths. Who in the universe does not possess a tiny portion of the truth?' (OC 4, 204).

An obvious conclusion to draw from all this is that a wider perspective on the truth can be obtained by putting different points of view together – precisely the point that Ortega makes: 'each individual, each generation and each epoch turns out to be an irreplaceable instrument of knowledge. The whole truth (*verdad integral*) can only be obtained by joining up what I see with what my neighbour sees and so on . . . The absolute all-embracing truth is arrived at by weaving together everyone's partial viewpoints' (OC 3, 202). This notion, of course, is not particularly novel, and I think that José Luis Molinuevo, for one, misses some of the point in implying that this is as far as Ortega's account of truth goes (p. 94).

Better and worse perspectives

More interesting, however, is the confrontation of the question as to how we are to decide whether some truths are more all-embracing than others. All of us, it will be remembered, have some truth to tell, and the relativist would say that there is no way of deciding between different truths. Ortega, too, has to say it is impossible for anyone to make an error. After all, if I am a sieve in a current of water representing reality then everything I catch is necessarily a part of that reality.

However, we have also seen him hinting that not all sieves are of the same configuration – some catch more than others. So although I cannot make an error, I can have access to truths that are more or less extensive. The extent of the truth to which I have access will depend upon my perspective – i.e. where I am, who I am and how I approach the world around me. If we want to continue talking of error, then, we must talk in terms of *errors of perspective* – the fact is that some perspectives are more fruitful than others: 'only certain types of existence include the optimum conditions for the most adequate knowledge' (OC 3, 407). As Ortega writes in *¿Qué es filosofía?*: 'There are those who see more than others, and those others cannot realistically do anything other than accept that superiority when it is in evidence' (OC 7, 341).

This sentiment clearly constitutes a rider to the apparently democratic implications of 'weaving together everyone's partial viewpoints', observed above. Once again Ortega's philosophy informs his sociology and Antonio Elorza accurately comments that, 'one can extrapolate that in the construction of the truth beginning with individual perspectives – truth being the sum of such perspectives – the perspectives of the select minority are those which really count in a positive sense (1984: 139). The question, nevertheless, is not the traditional one of how to decide between competing truths, but how to decide between different perspectives. To this question we now turn our attention.

With reference to the billiard-ball metaphor which we looked at earlier, it will be recalled that the 'conscious subject' (moving ball) comes into contact with reality (stationary ball) and such contact causes reality to 'release' one of its qualities – in the case of the billiard ball, its springiness. In the present context we would say that the 'conscious subject' with the best perspective will have more reality 'revealed' to it than such a subject with a less adequate perspective. How the world appears to me, then is dependent upon the point of view which I bring to bear. This, precisely, defines the fundamental importance of perspective. On this reading, reality is not 'independent of our point of view'. What must be remembered is that what we call things are not characterised as 'in themselves', but rather 'for me': they have perspective built into them. The trick is to develop a point of view which will persuade reality to give up as many of its secrets as possible. Now what might such a perspective look like?

The first feature of such a perspective is that it must function as an integrator of other, what Ortega calls 'incomplete' truths. Let us take the truths obtained by science – as does Ortega – as examples of these incomplete truths and then see how they might be made more all-embracing. He says that scientific truths are characterised by their exactitude, but that they achieve this rigour at the cost of leaving aside the 'ultimate, decisive questions' (OC 2, 601). The world with which physics (for example) deals is, necessarily, the world to which the aims and methods of physics respond adequately. But Ortega's point is that that is not the only world there is – in other words, the truths that physics tells are the truths of physics, but there are other truths to tell as well.

The perspective that science adopts, then, is one possible perspective among others – or one possible kind of sieve among others. As such, it will 'catch' its proportionate form and content of reality. But it is an essentially limited perspective, if only in the sense that it leaves unasked and unanswered such fundamental questions as, 'Where did the world come from and where is it going? . . . What is the essential meaning of life?' (OC 2, 602), and so on. Moreover, as we know, Ortega believes that it is 'psychologically impossible to give up the desire to have a complete notion of the world, an integral idea of the Universe' (OC 2, 601).

Bearing in mind the necessity we have to pose these ultimate questions and thus to seek answers to them, it is possible to adopt an inadequate perspective relating to them. Thus a physicist, for example, might be led to believe that the perspective of physical science was sufficient and adequate to deal with those questions which Ortega feels to be beyond the purview of physics. This would result in physicists doing damage to the facts they have before them in the attempt to force them into a perspective which simply is not built to contain them. This would be an *error of perspective*.

Over against this Ortega demands that the perspective respond to 'how things are' (OC 3, 164), which means that 'We need a complete perspective which contains foreground and background and is not mutilated' (OC 2, 602). One imagines, incidentally, that Ortega would argue against a confusion of a 'complete perspective' with an 'absolute perspective'. The latter is an impossible perspective, while the former is that perspective which is true both to itself and its object. The meaning of this will become clear as the chapter progresses. What, then, is this 'complete perspective'?

Ortega provides us with a clue when he says that our primary 'destiny' is not one of contemplation *per se* but rather 'contemplation from the point of view of life' (*interés vital*). In other words, feelings, necessities and preferences, far from being obstacles to understanding, are part of the equipment we must bring to bear on such understanding (OC 3, 406). Indeed in *La deshumanización del arte* he suggests that 'pure' contemplation is impossible:

Pure contemplation does not, and cannot, exist. If we confront the universe without any concerns we will never manage to see anything well because the number of things with an equal right to our attention is infinite. There would be no reason for settling on one point rather than another, and our disinterested eyes would wander here and there, sliding around the universal landscape with neither order nor perspective, incapable of settling on anything.   (OC 3, 405)

Our vision cannot be 'disinterested', then, because if it were we would never be presented with anything other than a blur, a confused jumble of objects. The most all-embracing truth will only be accessible to those who bring to bear – and are faithful to – a 'perspective from the point of view of life' (*perspectiva vital*). Recast in terms of the sieve analogy, it might be said that we must reshape our perspective such that it becomes the finest and the widest possible sieve – i.e. a perspective which is our whole life. Pure reason for Ortega represents only a partial perspective on the world, and as such will only reveal a partial reality. Pure reason attempts to 'bracket off' feelings and preferences as anathema to its enterprise – which they are. Ortega's point, though, is that the maximisation of the scope of our perspectives will only be achieved if every aspect of our condition as human beings is brought to bear, and not solely the capacity to reason.

An illustration of Ortega's point might be the position of the tourist visiting a foreign country. It is commonly recognised that an eight-week contemplation of a country by a tourist is as nothing – in terms of understanding that country – compared to a similar period spent working there. Why? Because working in the country involves one in living – as far as is possible – the lives of the people there. No matter how diligent one is, the contemplative tourist only ever scratches the surface of society without penetrating its depths. People who work there, on the other hand, are forced to bring every facet of their life to bear on their situation. This maximises the breadth and depth of their perspective and they are rewarded with a more profound understanding of the community in which they live owing to a heightening of their 'absorbent and receptive capabilities' (OC 3, 406).

This is clearly Ortega's point in a section of *La deshumanización del arte* entitled 'Unas gotas de fenomenología' (Some drops of phenomenology). He describes a man on his death-bed, attended by his wife, a journalist, an artist and a doctor. Each person relates to the event from a different point of view and each, therefore, has a different story about 'reality' to tell. Ortega asks, 'Which of those multiple realities is the real, authentic one?' (OC 3, 361). He suggests that one of the four perspectives is the presupposition of the other three making sense to us: 'If there was no one who had completely surrendered their self to living the agony of the dying man, the doctor would not bother with him, readers would not understand the journalist's inadequate gestures at describing the event and the artist's picture of a man on his death-bed surrounded by mourners would be unintelligible to us' (OC 3, 363). On this reading, the authentic reality is that which is lived: 'on the scale of realities, lived reality has a peculiar primacy which obliges us to see it as "the" reality *par excellence*' (*ibid.*). With human life itself established as the radical reality (chapter 8), Ortega further suggests here that the richest perspective we can take on reality is that which represents the point of view of life.

It should be clear from all of this that it is simply an error to suggest that for Ortega there is 'no authoritative and independent criterion' for deciding between various concepts or belief systems, or between ways of thinking in general. On the contrary, he says that the perspective on reality which we must adopt is dictated by the inexhaustible complexity of reality itself. The perspective has to be as rich as possible; therefore it would be counter-productive wilfully to amputate a part of us which could lead to such a widening of perspective. Pure reason is a perspective, but only a partial one. Its error, according to Ortega, lies in committing just such a wilful amputation by defining as obstacles to knowledge those facets of our existence – feelings, preferences, etc. – which Ortega considers to be essential to understanding. This is the fundamental meaning of his exhortation that 'The task of our time consists in making reason subject to vitality, finding its place within the biological and subordinating it to the spontaneous', and that 'Pure reason has to give way to "reason from life's point of view" (*razón vital*)' (OC 3, 178).

What truth is

All of the foregoing has been an attempt to describe Ortega's notion of perspectivism more accurately than has usually been the case in English-language studies. However, as suggested at the beginning of the chapter, none of this exhausts Ortega's reflections on the issue of truth. More specifically, it represents a formative period (approximately 1923–9) concerning his position as to how truth is to be arrived at. With the formalisation of the idea of individual human life as radical reality one finds Ortega beginning to address the question of truth in its most fundamental form – not, what is the truth?, but what is the nature of truth itself? To explain.

Ortega's account of individual human life as radical reality includes the notion that everything is found in human life and nothing can be considered apart from it – truth included. This simple observation has significant repercussions on the issue of what truth is. Just as philosophy has a specific role to play, so truth has its function in the economy of life. Truth is thus a necessity of life and the truth of a statement or belief is, in Ortega's mature opinion, to be judged from the point of view of its efficacy in the economy of the individual life. Just what this means will be considered in a moment, but we can illustrate the basic point from his *La razón histórica* (1940) 'Lost in his circumstances and always having to do something to survive, man has to believe that that which he does makes sense, i.e. that it is correct . . . He has to make an effort to be right . . . This means, concretely and specifically, that fundamental concepts are not self-derived from the intellect or pure reason but that they come about as necessities of life' (OC 12, 193).

From this perspective, truth is a function of life, is founded in it, and cannot sensibly be discussed outside of it. Truth is something that I have to have because it is uncomfortable for me to be wrong. My whole life is a struggle for security and peace with myself, and believing myself to have possession of the truth is a necessary presupposition of my feeling secure. Everything I do, I do 'so as to be happy' (OC 8, 86), and one imagines that I will know that I possess the truth when I am overwhelmingly content. At the most profound and fully human level, then, the truth of a statement or belief is to be judged by how far it results in serenity and contentment within the economy of an individual life. This is relatively simple, but complications arise when we consider just in what this happiness consists.

As a shorthand illustration of what he understands by serenity and contentment, Ortega often approvingly quotes Pindar's exhortation: 'Reach the point of being what you are' (OC 7, 337 for example). This is based on Ortega's understanding of the human condition as being defined by a fracture between that which I am (potentially) and that which I am (actually). Every thing has within it the possibility of plenitude, he writes early in his career – including the human being. Contentment comes with the merging of that which I actually am with that which I potentially am, and so the truth of a statement or belief is to be judged with reference to that potential. As Garagorri succinctly puts it, truth is 'that which I need to know so as to be that which I am' (1970: 104). Ortega himself writes:

the solution of a problem does not necessarily entail the discovery of a scientific law, but rather only to be clear with myself with regard to that which was a problem for me – suddenly to find one idea among the infinity of possible ones which clearly represents my actual and authentic attitude with respect to the problem. The substantial, basic, and in this sense, only problem is to fit myself to myself (*encajar yo en mi mismo*), to coincide with myself, to find myself.   (OC 4, 86)

Ortega is, of course, obliged at this point to give us some account of what this 'self' is: he needs a datum against which, and in function of which, various truths can be tested. This self turns out to be that which I potentially am. Further, he holds that the potential me is constituted by the 'project' which I am. My life, he asserts, has an unavoidable future moment and my present life is 'dragged' towards it: 'my *future* exerts pressure on the *here and now*, and from that pressure on circumstance springs my present life' (QC, 132). One proviso, the importance of which will shortly become apparent, is that while my being pulled towards the future is inevitable, my recognition of my project is not, and my fulfilment of that project – 'the life programme which we inexorably are' (*ibid*. p. 135) – is even less likely.

So far we have it that truth is that which I need to know so as to be what I am. Further, 'what I am' is to be understood as that which I *potentially* am – myself as project. The implication would seem to be that in order to judge the truth of a statement or belief, I would have to have some idea of what I, as project, am. The difficulty arises when we observe Ortega placing me-as-project in the pre-intellectual realm: 'I find myself being the project which I am before I think what project I am. What is more none of us has ever completely managed to think through the project that we are' (*ibid*. p. 134). The potential problem is that if I am to judge the truth of a statement or belief, I will have to have brought my project to the surface of consciousness. If I am not aware of what it is, then I will have no datum by which to judge truth and falsity.

Now Ortega does indeed suggest that there is a way of glimpsing the self-as-project: 'imagine oneself placed in various circumstances and note which ones seem to cancel or obliterate one's self' (*ibid*. p. 134). More specifically he writes: 'I feel that I am he who has to be a philosopher – I find in myself something like the necessity of being a philosopher. In other words, if I now imagine not being a philosopher, my future life appears to be a failure or (which amounts to the same thing), as if the "me" which I have to be did not happen, but was cancelled out' (*ibid*. p. 132). Each individual's project, then, is in principle discernible to the individual concerned. Nowhere, however – and this is the rub – does Ortega suggest that this bringing of the project to cognition is something which everybody does. The process of becoming aware of one's project is, on Ortega's reading, a matter of some effort, and he never suggests that everyone necessarily makes such an effort. The question then arises that if contentment is predicated upon being intellectually aware of one's project (and the consequent striving to achieve it), then does this mean that if one is not aware of one's project, one has no possibility of contentment?[1]

Now an affirmative answer to this question is at least intuitively acceptable because we can conceive of more or less permanently unhappy people. But even this cannot make sense of Ortega's position because if we concede that contentment is predicated upon my 'knowing' myself as project, then so must discontentment. I cannot know what discontentment is without, at some stage, having felt something like a state of contentment against which to 'check' my present, different, state. In other words, we arrive at the position that awareness of oneself as project seems to be a necessary precondition for experiencing happiness or unhappiness. This presents no problem if we can assert that we do all have some idea, however vague, of what we are as project but, as illustrated above, Ortega does not necessarily allow us this.

The difficulty, of course, is that most people do have some sense of happiness and unhappiness, even if they are unaware of themselves as project as Ortega defines it. The problem is exacerbated by the recognition that if we accept that contentment is unavailable to those whose project remains 'pre-intellectual', then truth, too, can have no meaning for them because, as was seen above, the truth of a statement or belief is to be judged by how far it allows me to 'coincide with' or 'find' myself. Again, we might want to object that this is unintelligible because our experience suggests that everyone has some idea of what truth is.

I think that Ortega's reply to these objections would take the following form. We know that for him there are different kinds of truth which, in turn, have different attributes. The truths sought by mathematicians, for example, *are* truths, but truths of a specific sort, one of whose attributes is that they are exact. But, writes Ortega, 'A truth might be very exact and yet be only a small truth' (OC 7, 316). Now Ortega can allow that the truths discovered by mathematicians

[1] Molinuevo comments that it may be that even if one is aware of oneself as project one is condemned to permanent unhappiness because nowhere does Ortega suggest that self-coincidence is realisable. (Molinuevo: 161).

will make them happy as mathematicians, but not necessarily as human beings, because there are questions which human beings ask which mathematics cannot answer. The exact truths of physics and mathematics may constitute steps on the way to fully human contentment, especially if I am a professional physicist or mathematician. But, argues Ortega, physicists and mathematicians are also human beings who live lives *within which* they do physics and mathematics. The truths of science may satisfy human beings as scientists, but such truths can never provide them satisfaction as human beings precisely because they operate within well-defined limits. In the same way in which physics, as activity, is embedded in life and presupposes it, so the truths of physics – adequate and functional and capable of generating contentment within their prescribed territory – need to be embedded in 'truth from the point of view of life'. As he expresses it in *¿Qué es filosofía?*: 'We can see here two clearly contrasted types of truth: the scientific and the philosophical. The former is exact but insufficient, and the latter is sufficient but inexact'.

From this point of view, Ortega is not committed to denying some notion of contentment and/or truth to those unaware of themselves as project. He would, however, hold that such people will not be in a position to experience the deepest and richest forms of truth and contentment. It seems clear that not everybody is subject to the feelings of discomfort generated by the gap between act and potentiality – only those who have reflected upon the project that they are will experience such feelings. *Authentic truth*, then, will be a function of the *authentic life*, and only inferior or partial truths will be available to those who live their lives inauthentically. This is the analogue of the situation described in chapter 7 where it was established that Ortega's early view that everyone always does philosophy was replaced by the notion that authentic philosophy is only done by those who do it authentically – i.e. radically and individually.

Ortega provides an apt conclusion to this chapter in his prologue to Brehier's *History of Philosophy*. Just as the contented life will be one that fulfils its potential and ought to be judged in those terms, so the truth of a philosophy should be judged by its adequacy in relation to its potential:

We do not think, nor do we have to think, that our philosophy is the definitive one, but rather we submerge it like any other in the historical flow of the changeable and corruptible. This means that we see *every* philosophy as mistaken – ours just the same as any other. But even while constituting an error, it is everything that it has to be because it is the authentic way of thinking of each epoch and each philosopher. The historical perspective changes once again. We come around again to seeing the past as a history of mistakes, but this time with a crucial difference compared to what that meant up until the eighteenth century. As far as the absolutism of those men was concerned, the past was an error because they had possession of the ultimate truth. Past mistakes were converted into absolute mistakes upon coming into contact with absolute truth . . . But today we reclaim yesterday and *therefore* a philosophy is the correct one not when it is definitive – which is unimaginable – but when it carries past philosophies within it, like entrails, and discovers the 'movement towards itself' in those philosophies. (OC 6, 418)

Naturally, this sentiment acts as a reply to those who would accuse Ortega of possessing an account of truth as subjectivity. He would object that truth has to *satisfy*. One cannot 'stay in a truth' (OC 9, 364) which one feels to be inadequate, for the feeling of discomfort this generates is precisely what intellectual activity is intended to allay. The truth at which one arrives has to be 'abreast of the times' (*a la altura de los tiempos*). As he wrote to Victoria Ocampo in 1930:

A life hits the mark when it is lived towards, with and of the most funda-mental of whatever events and ideas are abroad in the world at that par-ticular moment. It is useless for you to be an admirable person if you do not live what is *fundamental* in your epoch. In order to achieve this, your life has to stop sliding across the world . . . it must, on the contrary, sink its teeth into it. (FOG C. 186 JK 85/99 19.2.30)

Conclusion

I have sought to demonstrate in this chapter that it is insufficient to describe Ortega's perspectivism simply as a variant of truth-relativism. He believes, it is true, that everyone has access to a por-tion of truth, but he does not believe that every truth is of equal value. The truth acquired will be related to the perspective from which it is obtained, and given that perspectives can vary in their width and profundity, so truth, too, will be more or less far-reaching and profound. He suggests that the widest perspective available is that provided by life itself, and we shall be pursuing the implications of this in the next and final chapter.

To the extent that perspectivism was developed by Ortega in the middle of his career, it does not represent his final word on the subject of truth. It will now be clear that the two metaphors of the sieve and the billiard ball which he uses to illustrate the notion of perspective both depend upon a separation of subject and object for their intelligibility. However, his formalisation of individual human life as radical reality, described in chapter 8, dissolves this separation. Radical truth cannot be based upon the separation of subject and object because that separation is no longer held by Ortega to be an accurate description of reality itself. In other words, in the same way in which talk of 'subject' and 'object', as independent of each other, amounts to a *theory* about reality rather than a description of what reality radically is, so any notion of truth based on that separation will be a theory about truth rather than a description of truth itself. If, as Ortega asserts, radical reality is indeed individual human life, then any answer as to what truth is must be grounded in that reality. On this reading, truth is not whimsical: it is something I need in order to achieve intellectual security and thus to feel at peace with myself. Further, Ortega defines the self as the potential self, or the project which I am. Thus, in the authentic human being, truth will be that which I need to know in order to become my potential self.

10

Razón vital – reason from the point of view of life

In chapter 8, Ortega's notion of individual human life as radical reality was established. Strictly speaking, what there fundamentally *is* in the world is subject and object engaged in a continual relationship defined by interdependence rather than independence. This perspective has considerable repercussions in terms of a discussion of the nature of those objects which we normally describe as 'things'. Of course, to put the point that way is already, on Ortega's terms, to be indulging in theory rather than pure description because 'things' in their radical reality cannot be discussed apart from the subject for whom they exist. Ortega does indeed discuss them in this way, but he would claim that his treatment is not innocent or gullible in that he attempts to describe what things are while always bearing in mind that they are 'nothing' without the subject for whom they 'are'. In other words, although we need to 'remove' the object from its relationship with the subject in order to discuss it, the subsequent discussion will always take place in view of the fact that a definitive feature of the object is, precisely, its relationship with and towards a subject. This is, so to speak, a practical exercise in Ortega's technique of 'un-thinking', and what is principally to be 'un-thought' in this case is the notion of the independence of subject and object. An object fundamentally and radically is what it is when it is part of the executive act which Ortega considers to be the stuff of radical reality. His intention, then, is to recapture – albeit theoretically and intellectually – what an object is when it is a part of that pre-intellectual relationship.

Ortega's opening gambit is that the Being of things (by which he understands that which they are) has traditionally been conceived in a static sense. In *¿Qué es filosofía?* he supports Descartes in his intuition that thought has a 'being which consists in mere "appearance", in pure potentially, in a movement of reflection', but then continues

163

that, 'like an ancient, like a Thomist scholar, he needs to grab at something more solid – cosmic being'. The result, Ortega concludes, is that he sees a 'being-thing (*ser-cosa*), a static entity' (OC 7, 396). By contrast Ortega proposes a reform of the idea of Being – a task in which he writes enigmatically in 1929 that 'several men in Europe have been engaged for some time' (OC 7, 394): 'You are invited then, to lose your respect for the most venerable, persistent and weighty concept which exists in the tradition of thought: the concept of being. I say "checkmate" to the being of Plato, Aristotle, Leibniz, Kant and, of course, to that of Descartes as well' (*ibid.*).

Ortega's position is that if objects are conceived of as static, independent 'things', we shall not have access to what they really are. Independence and stasis are qualities or features which philosophers have invented for objects and this invention prevents us from seeing them in their radicality. Stasis and independence amount to ideas about reality rather than qualities of reality itself. They are hypotheses which, in Ortega's opinion, need to be discarded in the light of his discovery of individual human life – the arena of the executive act – as *the* radical reality. Such hypotheses, far from enabling us radically to conceive reality, constitute a veil which prevents us from doing so.

What an object radically is, then, is that which it is when it is embedded in the executive act of which it is a part – the to-ing and fro-ing between subject and object: 'When I say of this electric lamp that it is a "thing", I have already jumped ahead of what the lamp primarily is – I have added hypothetical attributes to its original being. Basically, this lamp is nothing other than that which is now shedding light on me. Its being is nothing other than its exercising the function of illuminating me' (QC, 120). The lamp is that which it is in its immediate relation to the subject for whom it 'is'.

Clearly this means that the lamp can 'be' many things, and Ortega confirms this in *Unas lecciones de metafísica* by adding that it 'is that which sheds light and allows me to read, that which I turn on or off, that which costs the Faculty such and such amount of money' (OC 12, 70). 'Things' in their radical reality are what they are in terms of their action upon me and in this sense must be conceived of in a transitive rather than in a static fashion (OC 6, 768 fn). Ortega described this in 1940 as follows:

The decisive fact is that the radical feature of our relationship with things is only accurately expressed as the naked coexistence of the '*myself*' with *things*. The *one* is as real as the *other*: *me* as well as *things*. But it is just that now *being real* means something different and instead of meaning *independence*, as before, it now has the sense of the *dependence* of the one upon the other: being inseparable – a mutual being towards each other (*serse*). I am given over to things: they surround me, they sustain me, they hurt me, they rub up against me. There is nothing of this *consciousness*, *thought* or *cogitatio* between me and them. The primary relationship of man with things is not intellectual, it is not a taking notice of them, thinking them, or contemplating them. What more do we want? The primary relationship is a being in them and with them and, as far as they are concerned, actually to be an acting upon me.   (OC 12, 180–1)

Objects do not consist, therefore, in their independence, but in their interdependence and action upon a subject. More specifically, as radical reality is not so much human life in general, but the life of each and every one of us, objects consist in their interdependence with and action upon me. Things radically are what they are for me.

Without wishing to labour the point, I shall conclude this description of interdependence with an extract from Ortega's *Commentario al 'Banquete' de Platón* (Commentary on Plato's *Banquet*) of 1946 in which the Spanish language becomes the subject of experiment: an attempt by Ortega to describe in words and thought what things are before they are described or thought:

The being in itself and for itself of the world, separate from us and with no relationship with any of us is a secondary, derived, interpretative and hypothetical being. The fundamental meaning of being is being-towards-us (*sernos*). At the same time, and whether we like it or not, each one of us is-to-himself (*se-es . . . a sí mismo*). It is not that this flower is for us because we see it now or because yesterday we thought of it, as subjectivist idealism believed. In that case we would not be talking about the flower but about a 'vision-of-the-flower' or a 'thought-of-the-flower'. The truth is the opposite of that: to perceive the flower or to think of it is to have this flower as flower being towards us (*estarnos siendo esta flor efectivamente esta flor*), even though in different aspects of its reality. This flower is towards us, or towards us it is-flower (*flor-es*). Its being is its 'flowering-towards-us' ('*florear-nos*') or its 'blooming-towards-us' ('*florecer-nos*'). Vice versa, this implies that *I am towards* this flower when I see it, smell it, imagine it, think it or wish it was here. The world is towards us and we are towards the world – whether we like it or not. Only, because I am towards myself and in as much as I am towards the world I am, strictly speaking, towards myself, towards the world (*me soy al mundo*).   (OC 9, 768)

Facilities and difficulties

All of this, however, is no more than general description, so to speak, of the relationship between subject and object – it is not a description of what that relationship actually consists in. An understanding of the difference will be aided by reference to Ortega's description of life as a 'task' (*quehacer*), or as a challenge to accomplish. In this context objects, as 'things' which I encounter in my life, must be described in terms of their function within life itself and in view of the fact that life is characterised as a task.

While giving his course, *Unas lecciones de metafísica*, Oretega began a class with a quotation from Sir Arthur Eddington in which the scientist is discussing the nature of the table he has in front of him in the light of physics' latest discoveries. Eddington refers to the common-sense view that the table is a 'thing' which has 'substance' and whose basic qualities are revealed by touching it, looking at it, smelling it, and so on. Then Eddington describes his 'scientific table' which modern physics assures us is 'practically a perfect vacuum' (OC 12, 92). Eddington's conclusion (in his own words) is as follows: 'It is clear that thanks to some delicate experimentation and rigorous logic, modern physics assures us that my scientific table is the only one which is really there' (OC 12, 94).

For Eddington the 'real' table is that which physics says it is: a collection of atoms, sub-atomic particles and the proportionately enormous space surrounding them. The real table is not that which we touch or smell, but that which the mental and experimental equipment of modern physics reveals it to be. This, clearly, will not be good enough for Ortega because it makes no reference to the function of the table within the economy of the individual life – precisely that which he believes will describe what the table really is. He suggests that the primary table is neither the common-sense one nor the scientific one. The table, he continues,

has no being in itself: it is there as an element in my life making it either easier or more difficult. It is either useful to me or an obstacle to me; it either helps me or deviates me from my aim. It might be said that the being of this table lies in helping me. However, what if I have to run because there is a fire? The table gets in my way. And even that being – i.e. as a facility or difficulty – is not the table itself because its being depends on what I have to do: writing or running away, for example. (OC 12, 95)

What the table is depends both on my relationship with it and how it functions as an instrument within the field that is the task that is my life. My circumstance, from this point of view, is not constituted by 'things' but by facilities and difficulties, and this is what 'things' radically are. By 1947 and the publication of *La idea del principio en Leibniz*, Ortega has introduced the Greek term *pragmata* to describe what 'things' are:

In their primary relation to man things do not have Being but rather they consist in objects which affect practicability (*practicidades*). From some remote past the Greeks preserved a very appropriate term to describe this . . . *pragmata* . . . The electric light in whose glow I am writing these lines consists in its shedding light on me or in leaving me in the dark when I most need it; in my switching it on and off, in my having it set up, in my paying the bill for the electricity it consumes, etc. etc.   (OC 8, 234)

According to Ortega, the world is neither solely difficult nor solely easy, but rather a combination of the two. Our primary sense of the world, however, is that it is hostile. This sense is the presupposition of our noticing that the world exists and, indeed, that which generates the activity of philosophy. On a number of occasions he says that in a world in which nothing was ever a problem, 'it would never occur to me to think about anything' (OC 12, 80). Ortega asserts that in order to distinguish between myself and everything else around me, my circumstance must occasionally present me with difficulties. If I wanted to pass by a table, for example, and the table simply dissolved in front of me, then it would appear as a mere extension of me. Thus if everything were pure facility there would be no world for me to call 'world': my surroundings would merge with me and would be indistingushable from me. Ortega's conclusion is that our primary notice of the world is its constitutive hostility. But he also observes that if the world were only hostile 'human life would be impossible' (OC 9, 208). The world being neither solely hostile nor solely pleasurable, Ortega concludes that it is a mixture of the two.

Towards a 'reason from life's point of view'

'Things', then, can never be accurately described so long as they are abstracted from that concrete radical relation between subject and object which is my life. What 'things' are can only be accurately assessed by placing them in the context of an individual life. Now it ought not to have escaped notice that both truth (cf. chapter 9) and 'objects' have come in for a certain amount of redefinition in the context of Ortega's metaphysics. The cause of these redefinitions is the same in both cases: the abandonment of the distinction between subject and object or, rather, the assertion that such a distinction is a feature of a theory about reality rather than a description of reality itself. In turn, reality itself is conceived by Ortega to consist in a to-ing and fro-ing, or a mutual being-towards (*serse*), of subject and object. This purely immediate relationship is the field of the executive act, and a series of such executive acts is what constitutes human life. In other words, the *theory* which advances mutual independence of subject and object is rejected in favour of what is held to be a *description* of their mutual dependence. Further, Ortega observes that this mutual being-towards is what we normally call human life.

Now, having established what he considers to be a novel form of radical reality, Ortega believes that he is in a position to show that other concepts and beliefs based on the old notions are to be found wanting. A conception of truth, for example, which is founded on the myth of the independence of subject and object will itself be problematic. Truth, on Ortega's reading, can only properly be described within the context of the to-ing and fro-ing of subject and object – i.e. human life. The redefinition of what truth is is a result of placing truth in the context of human life as radical reality. We have seen in the first part of this chapter that precisely the same operation is performed on 'things' or 'objects'. In other words truth and objects have been described in their radical reality according to Ortega by placing them in the context of the individual human life. This operation precisely describes that method or that type of reason which he calls *razón vital*, or 'reason from life's point of view'. By conducting our enquiry into Ortega's notions of what truth is and what objects are we have stumbled upon an understanding of that type of reason which has become the hallmark of Ortega's philosophy: 'reason from life's point of view'.

'Reason from life's point of view'

Things are what they are, writes Ortega, when we live them' (OC 12, 66) and this is because 'it is clear that everything that happens to man happens to him in his life and is thus converted into a fact of human life. That is to say that the true being or the reality of that fact is not that which it appears to be in itself as a brute, isolated event, but rather what it means in the life of that man' (OC 4, 18).

According to Ortega different sorts of reasons are necessary for different sorts of tasks. The error made by rationalists is to believe that everything is susceptible to what Ortega normally calls pure reason, but what he refers to in the following as 'pure thought' or simply 'thought'.

We must be absolutely clear that Ortega's criticism of rationalism is not a criticism of reason as such. His objection is aimed at those who hold that 'the texture of being perfectly coincides with the texture of thought' (OC 7, 325). Ortega's position is that 'being only coincides with thought in part – only certain objects behave in the same way as thought' (OC 7, 326). He continues: 'If we move up from mathematics to more complex subjects – the material of physics, organic life, the life of the mind, social life, historical life – the amount of irrationality or impenetrability to pure thought increases' (OC 7, 327).

Ortega suggests the need for a more all-embracing tool for the study of each complexity than that provided by pure thought or the reason of mathematics. He notes that Henri Bergson called this tool 'common sense', while Ortega announces that he calls it 'reason from life's point of view', 'for which a large number of subjects which were irrational as far as the old, conceptual or pure reason are concerned, become rational' (*ibid.*). The position is neatly expressed in a letter to Paul Hazard, preserved in the Fundación Ortega y Gasset in Madrid and which I believe to have been written between 1936 and 1939:

There are forceful reasons for fearing that if reason *is only* that which it has been since the time of Descartes up to the present day, i.e. the reason of mathematics and physics, then we can take the rational epoch of man as finished. However, if we preserve sufficient calm amidst the distress of the present and analyse properly and in detail the character of this lack of confidence, we find that it constitutes the root of the postulation of a new faith in a new form of reason, capable of dealing with human problems just as they are presented to us and without any naturalistic preconceptions. Philosophy's present task is to describe this new type of reason. It seems that philosophy – which fortunately has never been a science – has never had a more authentic occupation than that of defining new faiths. That is why my entire philosophical enterprise concludes with this scandalous proposition, this enormous piece of unorthodoxy: 'Man has no nature; he has only . . . history'.   (FOG C.203 JK 82/134 4.3.?)

The meaning of this final phrase will be discussed shortly, but for now it needs to be stressed that Ortega is suggesting that pure reason, or the reason of physics and mathematics, is perfectly valid in given areas, but that it is an error to suppose that it can be applied equally effectively to all types of problem. In *La idea del principio en Leibniz* he paraphrases Einstein in his support: 'Mathematical propositions are not valid in as much as they relate to reality, and in as much as they are valid they do not relate to reality' (OC 8, 105). Mathematical reason 'works' when it is applied to problems of mathematics, but Ortega insists that another type of reason is required for questions which explicitly relate to the activity of human beings in the world, such as: why do we do mathematics? If one wants to know what mathematics is in its radical reality, one must first accept that it is an activity which is done by some human beings for reasons which derive from the internal economy of their individual lives. In other words, the what and the why of mathematics only become intelligible when the activity is inserted into the context of an individual human life; and this insertion is precisely the exercise of what Ortega refers to as 'reason from life's point of view', or *razón vital*.

Ortega has often been accused of sacrificing rationality to irrationality on the strength of sentiments such as the following, expressed in the *El tema de nuestro tiempo*: 'Pure reason cannot replace life: the culture of the abstract intellect is not another self-sufficient life opposed to, and capable of dislodging, spontaneous life. *It is only a small island floating upon a sea of primary vitality*' (OC 3, 177). Ortega's intention here is neither to 'dislodge' pure reason itself, nor to claim that life is irrational. He simply says that pure reason has its place – that it has been founded in human life for specific problem-solving purposes. The 'sea of primary vitality' is opaque to pure reason and requires a different sort of reason to render it intelligible: this is *razón vital* or 'reason from life's point of view'.

Translating *razón vital*

A word ought to be said at this point about what some might regard as an idiosyncratic translation of Ortega's term *razón vital*. Invariably this has been rendered in English as 'vital reason'. From the shortest English monograph, through translations of the works of the best-known exponent of Ortega's life and philosophy, Julián Marías, to authorised translations of the works of Ortega himself, all seem to have agreed that 'vital reason' is the best rendering available of *razón vital*. Alan Pryce-Jones commented to *The Listener*, indeed, that he found himself 'forced' to translate *razón vital* as 'vital reason' (22 November 1951, p. 891). I do not agree, and my basic objection to the consensus is the following: it does not make sense in modern English. Although the word 'vital' in English can still mean 'full of life and force' or 'necessary for life', its primary meaning is that of 'very necessary' or 'of the greatest importance'. To this extent, 'vital reason' simply does not convey the immediate sense of *razón vital*, and is therefore inadequate as a translation.

In opting for 'reason from life's point of view' as a better rendering I have been influenced by the presence of Ortega's perspectivism in his notion of *razón vital*. *Razón vital* simply is 'reason from life's point of view', in the same sense as Ortega would argue that mathematical reason is reason from the point of view of mathematics. To this extent, it might be objected that what was intended as a translation has turned into a definition, to which I would reply that the definitional content is indeed greater than in the original, but that this disadvantage is far outweighed by the better sense that is conveyed. I am aware, too, of the relative clumsiness of the expression 'reason from life's point of view', but as Mary Warnock has said in a different context, 'It is misleading and confusing to try to say what Heidegger says in German in the same number of English words. In the nature of the case we shall need more' (1979: 50). I firmly believe that if in our particular instance intelligibility has to be bought at the cost of style, then the exchange rate is a good one.

Historical reason

By 1935, Ortega is referring to 'reason from life's point of view' as also being a 'historical reason' – *razón vital e histórica* (OC 6, 23). Some commentators have implied that the various adjectives Ortega attaches to 'reason' all mean more or less the same thing (e.g. Garagorri, 1970: 122), and although this might be persuasively argued in the case of 'living reason', or *razón viviente*, I think that the use of *historical* reason signals a change of emphasis which it would be a mistake to ignore.

In the first place, the date around which Ortega begins to make more consistent use of 'historical reason' is biographically significant. The chronology surrounding Ortega's reading of Wilhelm Dilthey (chapter 7) has already been explained, and it was suggested that he acquired a sense of history from the German philosopher which he had never had before. This made a substantive difference to his reflections on the question of what philosophy is and why some human beings do it.

Secondly, this encounter with history affected his notion of the nature of 'reason from life's point of view'. The affirmation that 'man has no nature, only history' (OC 6, 41 and 12, 237) and that 'life is always a place and a date' (OC 12, 76) led Ortega to the conclusion that life, as a concept, constitutes the general structure of existence within which concrete historical events take place: 'If we say that man always lives according to certain beliefs, we express a truth which is a theorem of the Theory of Life. But that truth says nothing about reality – indeed it will remain unreal as long as it does not make concrete the various beliefs from which man lives' (OC 6, 396–7). The general 'theory of life', then, is akin to an algebraic formula which needs to be filled in with numbers.

'Reason from life's point of view' amounts to an abstract description of the reason which needs to be exercised in the context of 'the things which surround man' (OC 8, 104) but, because the life of human beings is historical, the concrete use of that reason must itself be historical. It will be seen shortly that historical reason appears to be something more than the mere 'filling out' of the conclusions reached by 'reason from life's point of view'.

As far as I am aware, however, the first formal expression of this second principle comes with the publication of *La historia como sistema* (*History as a System*), and in the following extract Ortega illustrates precisely in what he considers the practice of historical reason to consist. He begins by asking what we have to do to find out 'why we are as we are', and answers:

Simply by recounting (*contar*), by narrating (*narrar*) that *before* I was the lover of this and that woman, that *before* I was a Christian; that the reader, of his own accord or under the influence of other men of whom he knows, was an absolutist, a caesarist, a democrat, etc. In a word the clarifying reasoning here, the *reason*, consists in narration. As against the pure reason of physics and mathematics, then, there is a narrative reason. In order to understand something human, whether it be personal or collective, it is necessary to tell a story. This man or this nation does such and such a thing and is the way he or it is *because* before they did this or that other thing and were of such and such a type. Life only becomes relatively transparent in the light of *historical reason*.   (OC 6, 39–40)

Historical reason is therefore a narrative reason, and as Ortega affirmed to the students of the Institute of Humanities in Madrid in 1949–50:

> narration is a form of reason in the most superlative sense of the word – a form of reason both alongside and contrasted with the reason of physics, mathematics and logic. In fact this is historical reason, a concept coined by me many years ago. It is as simple as 'good morning'. Historical reason, which consists in neither induction nor deduction but simply in narration, is the only reason capable of making sense of human realities because the make-up of these realities is historical, is *historicity*.
>
> (OC 9, 88–9)

Ortega evidently considered his 'discovery' of historical reason to be of great importance. For example he wrote to a Mr Ermengern in Belgium that: 'You will find the most important foretaste which I have given my thought on 'reason from life's point of view' under the title *History as a System*' (FOG C. 203 JK 54/134 18.11.37). And in 1940 he introduced a significant change to what was the culminating and definitive phrase of *El tema de nuestro tiempo* and which read: 'Pure reason has to give way to "reason from life's point of view" ' (OC 3, 178). By 1940 this has changed to: 'Pure reason has to be replaced by a narrative reason' (OC 12, 237). The relevant question here is: has Ortega progressed very far in apparently 'substituting' narrative reason for 'reason from life's point of view'?

This is not the place to embark upon a lengthy discussion of the relative merits of these two forms of what Ortega would claim to be the same type of reason, although a full treatment of his philosophical thought would be incomplete without it. His development of historical reason places him firmly in an interesting tradition which includes Jean-Paul Sartre, with his 'true novel' about Gustave Flaubert. The emphasis on the historicity of the human being is invaluable, but the dangers of bordering on banality are considerable, especially if no great care is taken as to how the story is to be told.

Examples of the use of historical reason abound in Ortega's work: for example, essays on Velázquez, Goya and Mirabeau, and a dissertation in his *La idea del principio – Leibniz* on why the word 'liver' (*hígado*) means what it means today. But in each case it is hard to escape the conclusion that he has simply 'told a story' without any account of a method which would cause us to take any more notice of his story than anyone else's. To this extent his stories carry less persuasive weight than they might have done had Ortega turned his mind to developing something like a method. Alongside Jean-Paul Sartre's biography of Gustave Flaubert, for example, with it's complex dialectic between individual and family, history and class, Ortega's stories come across as rather naive. Ortega never attempted anything like Sartre's *Question de méthode* and the results are consequently all the poorer. Hayden White quotes from *Sobre la razón histórica* (*Historical Reason*) to make the point: 'man is as he is because *yesterday* he was something else. Therefore, to understand what he is today we have only to relate what he was *yesterday*. That is enough, and here we have, come to light, just what we are doing here. This narrative is "historical reason" ' (*Times Literary Supplement* 31 January 1986, p. 110). Ortega's failure to give an adequate account of how these narratives are to be written is the reason for his inability to proceed into the interesting areas which are only gestured at in this kind of formulation.

Put another way, Ortega's notion of 'narrative reason' raises the hermeneutical problem of 'understanding from within'. While it is true to say that his instructions for arriving at such an understanding in the context of the specificity of an individual life or an individual word are vague, it should be noted that he does confront in more detail the issue of understanding an age. It is this investigation which produces his famous – or infamous – theory of generations. This theory is Ortega's key to unlocking the hermeneutic conundrum: 'The method of generations allows us to view human life from within itself in all its presentness (*actualidad*)' (OC 5, 40).

Building on his idea, previously discussed, that every date in history has its repertory of beliefs, Ortega argues that different generations living at that date refer to those beliefs in different ways. Broadly speaking, young people inhabit a world 'made' for them by the previous generation, but when they reach the age of twenty-five they begin to 'live it' of their own accord and make modifications to it. More specifically, Ortega claims that at any one moment three generations are historically operative, each with a different perspective on the world. It is this conclusion, based, on the elementary observation that human beings are born and then will die, that provides us with history: 'Thanks to this internal disequilibrium, [history] moves, changes, rolls and flows. If all of our contemporaries were the same age, history would come to a dead stop, petrified in one final and definitive form, with no possibility of radical change' (OC 5, 38).

The most active generation, writes Ortega, in terms of historical change is that which covers the age range of thirty to sixty years. More specifically still, he identifies two distinct stages within this range – 'each one of fifteen years: from thirty to forty-five, a period of gestation or creativity and argument: and from forty-five to sixty, a period of command and prevalence' (OC 5, 49). He adds three further generations to these two (0–15, 15–30 and 60–75) to arrive at a total of five.

This structure enables us, in Ortega's opinion, to deduce the 'ideas of epoch' or the 'spirit of the age' (OC 5, 35) and the way in which they change, because 'historical reality is substantially constituted at any one moment by the lives of men between thirty and sixty years old' (OC 5, 48). His recipe is to identify a period when human life radically changed, and then to isolate the decisive generation by isolating the decisive individual (or individuals) of the period. He chooses the 'Modern Period' as an example (whose maturity he identifies as having occurred between 1600 and 1650), and establishes Descartes as the 'decisive innovator' (OC 5, 52). Given his generational structure, described above, he only then needs to identify the date when Descartes was thirty years old – 1626 – and he has a nodal point from which to construct a table of generations within which to place individuals.

It should be stressed that this table is strictly constructed: the only people belonging to the generation of 1626 are those reaching the age of thirty between seven years before and seven years after that date. Ortega notes, for example, that Thomas Hobbes was born in 1588 and therefore had his thirtieth birthday in 1618: one year before the generation of Descartes and therefore excluded from it.

Ortega himself asks the question that many have since asked of him: 'What does this mean? That mathematical necessity, with its characteristic stupidity and abstraction, has to legislate for historical reality?' (OC 5, 53). He answers his own question in the negative, claiming that his table of generations is open to reconstruction if the 'facts' do not fit the 'figures'. If, for example, it could be shown that Hobbes and Descartes had identical intellectual pretensions, then the generational series would have to be run back so as to include them both in the same generation. As it happens, claims Ortega, no such reconstruction is necessary in the case of Hobbes because he only 'almost' sees things in the same way as Descartes

(OC 5, 52–3). He writes that it is as though two people see the same piece of countryside, but that one sees it from slightly higher up than the other. He continues: 'This difference in level, from the point of view of life, is what I call a generation' (OC 5, 53).

Many have attempted to make history intelligible through the prisms of generations: Schlegel, Ranke, Comte, Dilthey and Mannheim to name just five. Ortega's theory is generally recognised as being the most extreme (some would say outlandish) of them all. This is principally because its imposition of biological rhythms on socio-historical phenomena is absolute and universal, whereas less ambitious theorists have held that generations of thought are produced within the historical process as a whole. Ortega's notion is open to a number of objections, three of which might be mentioned here: that he allows historical and social events no autonomy; that the carrying over of generational differences between individuals into large collectivities is fraught with problems of differentiation; and that collectivities themselves are allowed no space as historical actors in their own right. Hans Jaeger has commented that the 'grotesque ineptness of this thesis [of generations] prohibits any closer scrutiny' (1985: 282).

From his own perspective – that of opening up the 'spirit of an age' for observation – the essential difficulty for Ortega is one of arbitrariness: how is the nodal individual to be chosen? Most would agree that Descartes is an immensely important figure in the history of human thought, but why should he be chosen as the individual through which the subsequent history of Western thought should be viewed? Different individuals will produce different 'spirits of the age', and it is wholly unlikely that multiples of fifteen, beginning from a figure which is itself open to debate, will solve the hermeneutical problem which Ortega sets himself. Further, how are the 'slight' differences between Hobbes and Descartes to be calibrated? Once again, Ortega has no method at his disposal which would allow us to interpret the identifiable 'facts'.

Moving on from the theory of generations, it should also be noted that the object of knowledge is different for 'reason from life's point of view' and for historical reason, and this, incidentally, is another reason why Garagorri's implication that these two reasons amount to the same thing is misleading. In the case of the former Ortega is primarily intent on describing what things are in the context of individual life as radical reality, and thus what they themselves radically are. In the second case, the intention is to show how people, words or objects come to be as they are. To my mind, Ortega proceeded further and more fruitfully in the first case than he did in the second. This is not to say, however, that the second case represents anything like a dead end, and it would be of great interest clearly to define Ortega's place in the philosophical narrative tradition.

Be that as it may, he considers historical reason to encapsulate all other forms of reason and thus to be superior to them. He says in *Una interpretación de la Historia Universal*, a course given in the Institute of Humanities in 1948–9 on Arnold Toynbee, that: 'the truth is that historical reason is the basis, foundation and presupposition of the reason of physics, mathematics and logic which are no more than particular, specific and deficient abstractions of it' (OC 9, 89).

It is hard to know what he means by 'presupposition' here. In developing the notion of individual human life as radical reality in chapter 8, it was indeed intelligible that physics, mathematics and logic should be held to be dependent upon life and seen as activities which are undertaken within it. In this case, though, Ortega is not referring to the presuppositions of the thing itself but rather of the way in which it is carried out. He is not only suggesting that mathematics presupposes life but that mathematical reason presupposes historical reason. If this means that one cannot employ mathematical reason before one has employed historical reason then he is surely wrong: mathematicians do precisely that every day. If, however, he is implying that its superiority derives from its subject-matter then what he is saying becomes comprehensible, even if only in his own terms. Human life, he might argue, is presuppositionless reality, therefore the reason employed to understand it must, in principle, be equally fundamental. The foundational nature which Ortega claims for historical reason can only be justified by reference to its object of study – human life.

Conclusion

This last observation brings us full circle. Ortega's entire philosophical enterprise can be seen in terms of an attempt to found individual human life, the life of each and every one of us, as *the* radical reality. Once established as such, human life truly becomes the standard by which all things are measured. Philosophy, truth, the things we encounter around us, and even history itself – indeed anything with which we enter into relation – are seen in terms of their foundation and generation in human life.

In almost all cases this involves, in Ortega's opinion, a reappraisal of the most familiar notions. Philosophy, for example, is not now the result of some abstruse volition but is rather born of an internal necessity in the lives of some few people. It would indeed be a way of life for everyone if we could only all indulge in an authentic search for intellectual security. Truth is now only in special cases a question of the correspondence of what we think with what there 'is': Ortega has it recast in terms of a life-derived necessity – something which the internal economy of life itself 'demands' that we find. By the same token 'things' are what they are not when we perceive them or reflect upon them but when they are a part of that executive act which is the stuff of radical reality and which is pre-intellectual.

In 1916, Ortega wrote an article for the first number of *El Espectador* whose title and concluding words amount to a self-definition: he described himself as 'not at all modern but very twentieth-century' (OC 2, 23). In the context of this particular article his rejection of the 'modern' is a rejection of the nineteenth century in general (and the forms of thought on which he considered it to have been built), and of course positivism in particular. Seventeen years later, in 1933, he reflected during his course *En torno a Galileo* that the 1916 formula was rather 'petulant and affected', but that as time had gone by it had come to seem more and more correct (OC 5, 57). By this time, Ortega had developed a more detailed analysis of the 'modern', and it is clear that in rejecting its suppositions he believed himself to be the vehicle for a new form of thought, the consequences of which would be no less far-reaching than Descartes' *cogito, ergo sum*.

The implications of this self-assessment are hard to understand without some idea of what Ortega means by a historical crisis: the kind of change which a civilisation might undergo only two or three times every thousand years, and which he believed his generation to be living through. We are acquainted with Ortega's notion, explained in the last chapter, that every historical period has a repertory of beliefs which amount to its intellectual foundations. Moreover, it was noted that modifications to these beliefs are brought about by the different perspectives which new generations bring to bear on social and intellectual life. Not all modifications, however, are of the same consequence: Ortega seeks to distinguish between 'changes in the world' and a situation in which 'the world has changed' (OC 5, 64). The latter is the kind of alteration which happens very infrequently. It is an alteration brought about by a given generation's realisation that the most fundamental of a society's beliefs are now ineffective. Put differently, Ortega would say that a historical crisis requires two ingredients: first, a set of received opinions and projects which are developed 'authentically' by a generation which had need of a radical reorientation of beliefs; and second, a new generation of 'authentic' individuals for whom the received opinions and projects are fundamentally inadequate for the purposes of the new age.

It was Ortega's belief that just such a change occurred some time around 1600 when 'a new form of life, a new man, arose – modern man' (OC 5, 56). The use of the word 'modern' here is no accident: once again Ortega is sketching out the beliefs against which he considered himself – as an 'authentic' thinker of the twentieth century – to be ranged. More specifically he claims that 'modern man' began by being 'Cartesian man', and more specifically still, modern man is defined by his faith in the potentialities of pure reason. The great change which took place around 1600 was that 'revelation' was found wanting as a source of intellectual security, and the modern age began when pure reason took its place: 'In it [the modern age] man made science, pure reason, serve as the foundation for his entire system of convictions' (OC 5, 66).

Now Ortega's belief was that the signs of crisis which he detected in the intellectual life of the sixteenth century were being repeated in the first third of the twentieth. For him, a study of the anatomy of the crisis which produced the hegemony of pure reason 'is of enormous interest because we live in a crisis-ridden epoch in which man, whether he likes it or not, has to make another great change of course' (OC 5, 56). In the same way in which revelation was succeeded by pure reason because of the failure of the former to do the work required of it given a new set of historical conditions, so the latter must now succumb: 'Is it not sensible to suspect that the present crisis is a result of the fact that the new position adopted in 1600 – the "modern" position – has exhausted all its possibilities and . . . has discovered its own limitations, he contradictions and its insufficiencies?' (OC 5, 56). In other words Ortega believed that after 300 years of intellectual dominance the bell was beginning to toll for pure, or scientific, reason.

Let there be no doubt that Ortega considered himself to be central to this 'change of course' which he believed humanity was about to undergo. He evidently reckoned himself to be the kind of authentic thinker capable of taking the new age by the scruff of the neck and placing it on the new set of intellectual foundations which it needed. Put simply, if revelation gave way to pure reason in the seventeenth century, then pure reason must now give way to *razón vital* – 'reason from life's point of view'. In 1933 he wrote: 'Over against revelation pure reason, or science, was erected. Today, over against pure reason, life itself claims dominance. That is to say that ''reason from life's point of view'' claims dominance because, as we have seen, to live is to have no option other than to reason in the face of inexorable circumstance' (OC 5, 67). Modernity's chief intellectual characteristic, for Ortega, was to view the world from the perspective of science; the twentieth century, he claimed, would learn to employ the perspective of life, and Ortega himself would show it the way.

He considered, then, that individual human life as radical reality and 'reason from life's point of view', or *razón vital*, were discoveries which amounted to a 'radical reform of philosophy' (OC 3, 200). In these last four chapters I have sketched the skeleton of his conception of such a reform, but do not pretend to have evaluated its status. The opportunity is there for an appraisal to take place and this final section of the present book will have served its purpose if it aids a decision as to the worth of such an undertaking.

Select Bibliography

Avineri, Shlomo. 1968. *The Social and Political Thought of Karl Marx*. Cambridge University Press.

Bachrach, Peter. 1972. *The Theory of Democratic Elitism*. University of London.

Barea, A. 1984. *La forja de un rebelde*, (3 vols.). Turner, Madrid.

Baroja, Pío. 1985. *El árbol de la ciencia*. Cátedra, Madrid.

Bayón, J. 1972. *Razón vital y dialéctica en Ortega*. Revista de Occidente, Madrid.

Ben-Ami, S. 1983. *Fascism from Above*. Clarendon Press, Oxford.

Blinkhorn, M. (ed.). 1986. *Spain in Conflict: 1931–1939*. Sage, London.

Bookchin, Murray. 1980. *Los anarquistas espanoles*. Grijalbo, Barcelona.

Bottomore, Tom. 1968. *Elites and Society*. Penguin.

Brenan, G. 1985. *El laberinto espanol*. Plaza and Janés, Barcelona.

Burke, Edmund. 1984. *Reflections on the Revolution in France*. Penguin.

Butt, J. 1978. *Writers and Politics in Modern Spain*. Hodder and Stoughton, Sevenoaks.

Carr, Raymond. 1980. *Modern Spain (1875–1980)*. Opus, Oxford.

Carsten, F. L. 1970. *The Rise of Fascism*. Methuen, London.

Cerezo Galán, Pedro. 1984. *La voluntad de aventura*. Ariel, Barcelona.

Chadbourne, Richard M. 1968. *Ernest Renan*. Twayne, New York.

Chamizo Domínguez, P. J. 1985. *Ortega y la cultura espanola*. Cincel, Madrid.

Descombes, V. 1980. *Modern French Philosophy*. Cambridge University Press.

Desvois, J. M. 1977. *La prensa en Espana*. Siglo veintiuno, Madrid.

Donald, James and Hall, Stuart (eds.). 1986. *Politics and Ideology*. Open University Press, Milton Keynes.

Durán, M. (ed.). 1985. *Ortega, hoy*. Universidad veracruzana, Xalapa, Mexico.

Eccleshall, R. et al. 1985. *Political Ideologies*. Hutchinson, London.

Elorza, Antonio. 1984. *La razón y la sombra*. Anagrama, Barcelona.

Ferrater Mora, José. 1956. *Ortega y Gasset: An Outline of his Philosophy*. Bowes and Bowes, London.

Flew, A. 1984. *A Dictionary of Philosophy*. Pan, London.

Garagorri, P. 1970. *Introducción a Ortega*. Alianza, Madrid.

Gibson, Ian. 1980. *En busca de José Antonio*. Planeta, Barcelona.

Guérin, Daniel. 1970. *Anarchism*. Monthly Review Press, New York.

Halliday, R. J. 1976. *John Stuart Mill*. Allen and Unwin, London.

Heywood, P. September, 1986. '*De las dificultades para ser marxista.*' *Sistema*, 74.

Jaeger, H. 1985. 'Generations in history: reflections on a controversial concept.' *History and Theory*, vol. 24, 1985, 273–92.

José Ortega y Gasset: imagenes de una vida 1883–1955. 1983. Ministerio de Cultura y Fundación Ortega y Gasset, Madrid.

Lalcona, Javier. 1974. *El idealismo político de Ortega y Gasset*. Edicusa, Madrid.

Langdon-Davies, J. 1937. *Behind the Spanish Barricades*. Secker and Warburg, London.

Lannon, F. 1987. *Privilege, Persecution and Prophecy: the Catholic Church in Spain 1875–1975*. Clarendon Press, Oxford.

Lichtheim, George. 1969. *A Short History of Socialism*. Fontana, London.

Livingstone, L. 1952. 'Ortega y Gasset's philosophy of art'. *Publications of the MLA*, 67, 609–54.

López-Morillas, Juan. 1981. *The Krausist Movement and Ideological Change in Spain, 1854–1874*. Cambridge University Press.

McClintock, R. 1968. *Ortega as Educator: An Essay in the History of Pedagogy*. Columbia University Press, New York.

Marías, Julián. 1960. *Ortega I: Circunstancia y vocación*. Madrid.

1983. *Ortega II: Les trayectorias*. Madrid.

1971. *Acerca de Ortega*. Revista de Occidente, Madrid.

Martínez Cuadrado, Miguel. 1983. *La burguesia conservadora (1874–1931)*. Alianza, Madrid.

Mill, John Stuart. 1980. *Utilitarianism, On Liberty and Considerations on Representative Government*. Dent, London.

Molinuevo, José Luis. 1984? *El idealismo de Ortega*, Narcea, Madrid.

Munoz Alonso, Adolfo. 1971. *Un pensador para un pueblo*. Almena, Madrid.

Ortega y Gasset, José. 1940. *Ideas y creencias*. Espasa Calpe, Buenos Aires.

1946–83. *Obras Completas*. Revista de Occidente, Madrid.

1974. *Epistolario*. Revista de Occidente, Madrid.

1981. *El hombre y la gente*. Alianza, Madrid.

1984. *Qué es conocimiento?* Alianza, Madrid.

Ortega, Miguel. 1983. *Ortega y Gasset, mi padre*. Planeta, Barcelona.

Ouimette, V. 1982. *José Ortega y Gasset*. Twayne, Boston.

Parry, Geraint. 1976. *Political Elites*. Allen and Unwin, London.

Payne, Stanley G. (ed.). 1976. *Politics and Society in Twentieth Century Spain*. New Viewpoints, New York/London.

Pérez Galdós, Benito. 1980. *Cánovas*. Alianza, Madrid.

Preston, P. (ed.). 1984. *Revolution and War in Spain, 1931–1939*. Methuen, London.

Redondo, Gonzolo. 1970. *Las empresas políticas de José Ortega y Gasset* (2 vols). Rialp, Madrid.

Rodríguez Huéscar, Antonio. 1982. *La inovación metafísica de Ortega: crítica y superación del idealismo*. Ministerio de Educacion y Cienca, Madrid.

1985. *Perspectiva y verdad*. Alianza, Madrid.

Silver. Philip W. 1978. *Fenomenología y razón vital*. Alianza, Madrid.

Solé Tura, Jordi and Aja, Eliseo. 1980. *Constituciones y períodos constituyentes en Espana (1808–1936)*. Siglo veintiuno, Madrid.

Tortella Casares, Gabriel, et al., 1901. *Revolución burguesa, oligarquía, y constitucionalismo (1824–1933)*. Labor, Barcelona.

Unamuno, Miguel de. 1973. *Del sentimiento trágico de la vida*. Losada, Buenos Aires.

Villacorta Banos, F. 1980. *Burguesía y cultura: los intelectuales espanoles en la sociedad liberal, 1808–1931*. Siglo veintiuno, Madrid.

Waldron, J. 1985. *Theories of Rights*. Oxford University Press.

Warnock, M. 1979. *Existentialism*. Oxford University Press.

The key for the correspondence which is kept in the Fundación Ortega y Gasset in Madrid works as follows: (1) the name of the Fundación (2) the number of the file (3) the number of the plastic card on which the letter is microfilmed (4) the date of the letter. Thus, FOG C. 204 JK 101/134 29.10.46 refers to file number 204, plastic card number 101/134, and date 29.10.46.

Index